KINGDOM LIFE

LIVING IN THE KINGDOM OF HEAVEN ON EARTH

RHONDA J. MEAD

ISBN 978-1-0980-5527-1 (paperback)
ISBN 978-1-0980-5528-8 (digital)

Christian Faith Publishing, Inc.
832 Park Avenue
Meadville, PA 16335
www.christianfaithpublishing.com

New Life Outreach
Holton, MI 49425 USA

Printed in the United States of America

Contents

Preface

The intention of this book is to stir you to search scripture to determine if what is presented is true. I trust this book will shake your theology and sift out the tradition of men. No denomination has a corner on the truth, whereas each denomination that embraces Jesus Christ as Lord has a piece of the puzzle. Together we form a picture of the body of Christ. During "the dispensation of the fullness of the times" (Ephesians 1:10, NKJV), the purification of the body of Christ will leave a beautiful, pure, and spotless bride who, with the Lord as her head, will reap the final harvest of the earth.

Every true believer is a vital member of the body of Christ. It is time to lay down our differences. When we embrace each other, we embrace Christ. As we embrace Christ through identification with His death, burial, resurrection, and ascension, we will be changed into His likeness. The body of Christ, functioning as a whole, while being conformed to His likeness, is the picture of the "mature man" of Ephesians 4:13. This mature body will be an expression of our Heavenly Father in the earth and will draw all men unto our head, who is Christ.

A key to individual maturation is the realization that we became citizens of the Kingdom of Heaven the day we were born again and that we mature as we learn to walk in kingdom principles. This book is designed to take you from the knowledge of *The Exchanged Life* (my previous book) to the vital experience of walking every moment of your life in identification with Christ.

I challenge you to read on. I dare you to open your heart to God and pray:

"Father, please forgive me if I have been narrow-minded. Forgive me for any spiritual pride and prejudice. Right now, I yield myself to You anew, so Your Spirit can lead me into all truth."

In the words of Jesus, Himself, to the Jews who had believed in Him, "If you continue in My word, then you are truly disciples of Mine; and you will know the truth, and the truth will make you free" (John 8:31b).

Introduction

The Kingdom of God or the Kingdom of Heaven (synonymous terms) has been covered with the dust of self-effort for hundreds of years. However, the time has come for the tablets of our hearts to be dusted off and prepared as a place for the King of Glory to rule and reign.

We desperately need to understand that we live in the Kingdom of God now, on this earth. The kingdom is an invisible realm, which although not seen, is more real than anything we can see with our natural eyes. The Kingdom of Heaven is not a far-off place but a spiritual dimension in which we already live, through our relationship with Jesus Christ.

This definition of the Kingdom of Heaven helps to clarify this truth. The Kingdom of Heaven is:

> The sovereign rule of God, manifested in Christ to defeat His enemies, with a people over whom He reigns, and a realm in which the power of His reign is experienced.[1]

[1.] Vine's Expository Dictionary of New Testament Words

The Truth Must
Be Revealed!

It is recorded in the book of 2 Chronicles that in the reign of King Josiah, the book of the law was discovered under layers of dust and rubble. Through years of disregarding God's word, His people had strayed from walking in His ways. In chapter 34, the king issued the following command:

> "Go, inquire of the LORD for me and for those who are left in Israel and in Judah, concerning the words of the book which has been found; for great is the wrath of the LORD which is poured out on us because our fathers have not observed the word of the LORD, to do according to all that is written in this book." So Hilkiah and those whom the king had told went to Huldah the prophetess, the wife of Shallum the son of Tokhath, the son of Hasrah, the keeper of the wardrobe (now she lived in Jerusalem in the second quarter); and they spoke to her regarding this. She said to them, "Thus says the LORD, the God of Israel, 'Tell the man who sent you to Me, thus says the LORD, Behold, I am bringing evil on this place and on its inhabitants, even all the curses written in the book which they have read in the presence of the king of Judah. Because they have forsaken Me and have burned incense to other gods, that they might provoke Me to anger with all the works of their hands; therefore My wrath will be poured out on this place and it shall not be quenched. But to the king of Judah who sent you to inquire of the LORD, thus you will say to him, Thus says the LORD God of Israel regard-

ing the words which you have heard, Because your heart was tender and you humbled yourself before God when you heard His words against this place and against its inhabitants, and because you humbled yourself before Me, tore your clothes and wept before Me, I truly have heard you,'" declares the LORD. "Behold, I will gather you to your fathers and you shall be gathered to your grave in peace, so your eyes will not see all the evil which I will bring on this place and on its inhabitants." And they brought back word to the king. Then the king sent and gathered all the elders of Judah and Jerusalem. The king went up to the house of the LORD and all the men of Judah, the inhabitants of Jerusalem, the priests, the Levites and all the people, from the greatest to the least; and he read in their hearing all the words of the book of the covenant which was found in the house of the LORD. Then the king stood in his place and made a covenant before the LORD to walk after the LORD, and to keep His commandments and His testimonies and His statutes with all his heart and with all his soul, to perform the words of the covenant written in this book. Moreover, he made all who were present in Jerusalem and Benjamin to stand with him. So the inhabitants of Jerusalem did according to the covenant of God, the God of their fathers. (2 Chronicles 34:21–32)

It had been so long since the children of Israel had cared to know the word of the Lord, that the book of the law was buried. They served man-made idols and did what seemed right in their own eyes. In the midst of this neglect, we see God waiting and longing for their hearts to turn back to Him.

In our day, we have continued on with religious form and tradition but have failed to walk in true kingdom life. For generations, we have neglected to study the truth regarding the Kingdom of Heaven. We have allowed misunderstandings of the kingdom and sentimental pictures of heaven to supersede a thorough study of biblical truth. Our carelessness in handling the Word of Truth on this subject has left the church of Jesus Christ in disrepair and discouragement.

The early church turned the world upside down—the effect of what they taught and lived still remaining. Yet, we as followers of the same Christ, filled with the same Holy Spirit, rarely affect a community, let alone the world. The majority of the church of Jesus Christ goes through the motions of church life as we know it, but few Christians understand His ways.

Likewise, few Christians understand the Kingdom of God as Jesus taught it. As we study the teachings of our Lord in the following chapters, we will need to let the dust of years of thinking and training roll off our hearts in preparation for anything new the Lord might have for us. This is not to suggest the entrance of any revelation differing from the written word of God but to expose the possibility that our preconceived mind-sets could block us from what God is trying to apply to our lives. For various reasons, we are much like the children of Israel who were familiar with God's acts but did not understand His ways.

Our quest then is to study the Kingdom of God as taught by the King Himself. We will attempt to not add to the word of God but will also strive to not leave anything uncovered. There awaits a new frontier before us!

When we receive Jesus as our Savior, we are translated, transferred, or transplanted from the domain of darkness into the Kingdom of His Beloved Son (Colossians 1:13). This means that when we are born again, we are already in the Kingdom of Heaven. We still live on this planet, but from new birth on, we are citizens of the kingdom, while at the same time aliens on this earth. As we proceed to study the Kingdom of God, the precept we will stand on is this:

> God's primary concern is not where we go when we die, but what kingdom we choose to live in today—eternity is a byproduct of that choice.

Where we spend eternity is not God's primary purpose in saving us. His eternal plan was to reverse the results of Adam's fall by bringing us into His kingdom, which then freed us from Satan's domain. Our Heavenly Father's original intent is to have many sons and daughters who are created in the image of His Son—sons and daughters who will rule and reign with Him forever on a new earth where righteousness dwells (2 Peter 3:13). We will continue to live in the Kingdom of Heaven as long as we trust in Jesus as our only hope of eternal life.

The Lord is ready to pour out His Spirit upon the earth unlike anything we have ever seen. In preparation for this outpouring, we need to study the principles of His kingdom like never before. These truths have the power to accelerate our transformation into His image and to turn societies upside down. We must abandon our 'methods' and 'programs' and allow Jesus to freely live His Life through us. Jesus said, "And I, if I am lifted up from the earth, will draw all men to Myself" (John 12:32). When His life is allowed to reign in our hearts—which will result in our lives changing—people will see Jesus in us and be drawn to Him, even as if He Himself were presently walking the earth.

There is more to your Christian walk than you are experiencing! God has a reality for you—on this earth—that few will ever taste of. "The Kingdom of God is at hand" (Mark 1:15). This realm is available for you to live in now, in preparation for eternity.

Chapter 1

The Kingdom of God Is at Hand

The time is fulfilled, and the Kingdom of God is at hand; repent and believe in the gospel.

—Mark 1:15

A correct understanding of the concept of the Kingdom of God, synonymous with the Kingdom of Heaven, is a necessary foundation for kingdom living. Dying and going to heaven is not the entrance to the Kingdom of God. Neither do we gain entrance to the kingdom upon Jesus Christ's Second Coming. The Kingdom of Heaven is only accessed through personal faith in the redemptive work of Jesus Christ and is entered simultaneously with new birth.

Jesus Brought Heaven to Earth

Jesus began His public ministry with the announcement that the Kingdom of Heaven had come to earth through His incarnation. In the first chapter of the gospel of Mark, He proclaimed, "The time is fulfilled and the Kingdom of God is at hand" (Mark 1:15). "At hand" is a reference to the Old Testament scriptures containing the promise of the coming Messiah. "The time is fulfilled" proclaimed that the Kingdom of God had come to earth. With this public statement, Jesus was claiming to be the long-awaited Messiah, as well as the vehicle through whom the kingdom had come to earth.

The church of Jesus Christ has taught the need for repentance and salvation throughout the centuries. Nonetheless, the importance of the first part of Mark 1:15, which is "the Kingdom of God is at hand," has rarely been emphasized. "At hand" means with us now—or in other words—as close to you as your own hand. *Strong's Hebrew and Greek Dictionary* describes "at hand" as "to make near" or to "come draw near." The Kingdom of Heaven was brought near to us through Jesus Christ, giving us the ability to draw near to a holy God. Through Jesus coming to earth as a man, the very presence of Almighty God came to permanently abide in this world.

The Presence of God Is the Essence of Heaven

Jesus brought the abiding presence of God to earth—first in Himself and then through the sending of the Holy Spirit to remain in His stead. The presence of God ushers in the Kingdom of Heaven, for the presence of God—who is Spirit (John 4:24)—is the essence of "heaven." When Jesus was caught up from the earth to sit at the right hand of the Father, the Kingdom of God continued on through the Holy Spirit's presence in the lives of the many-membered body of Christ. God the Father, God the Son, and God the Holy Spirit had a plan before the foundation of the world to bring the Kingdom of Heaven to earth.

When Jesus was baptized in the river Jordan and subsequently released into public ministry, He could proclaim the Kingdom of God had come. Since He functioned as a man filled with the Holy Spirit, He released the kingdom wherever He went. Jesus was yielded to the Father at all times, allowing the kingdom to flow continuously from His innermost being. Consequently, Jesus could boldly proclaim that the Kingdom of Heaven had come to earth—through Him.

Now having been questioned by the Pharisees as to when the Kingdom of God was coming, He answered them and said,

14

"The Kingdom of God is not coming with signs to be observed;
nor will they say, 'Look, here it is!' or, 'There it is!' For behold,
the Kingdom of God is in your midst." (Luke 17:20–21)

During His earthly ministry, Jesus humbled Himself as a man
and laid aside His rights as God. He walked this earth as a man completely yielded to the Holy Spirit—an example to us as to how we
should walk and could walk in His kingdom while living on this earth.

John the Baptist—Sent to Declare the Kingdom

John the Baptist, who was sent to prepare the way of the
Lord, proclaimed: "Repent, for the Kingdom of Heaven is at hand"
(Matthew 3:2). Jesus Himself proclaimed of John, "among those
born of women there has not arisen anyone greater than John the
Baptist!" (Matthew 11:11). This great prophet of God was given the
message that the Kingdom of God had come. Repentance and the
consequent forgiveness of sins are the entrance to the kingdom, but
these steps are just the beginning. It is no wonder that John was
willing to give his life for the proclamation of the gospel of the kingdom. He had received the glorious revelation that His kingdom was
actually coming to earth!

The expectation in John's heart of the coming kingdom is
expressed again in the seventh chapter of Luke. At this point in his
life, John the Baptist was imprisoned, had summoned two of his
disciples to go to Jesus, and had asked if Jesus really was the Christ.
There are many things that might have proven Jesus was the Messiah,
but Jesus specifically gave an account of signs and wonders singular
to the Kingdom of God. The following description in Luke records
Jesus' response to John's disciples:

When the men came to Him, they said, "John the Baptist has
sent us to You, to ask, Are You the Expected One, or do we look
for someone else?" At that very time He cured many people of
diseases and afflictions and evil spirits; and He gave sight to
many who were blind. And He answered and said to them, "Go

15

and report to John what you have seen and heard: the blind receive sight, the lame walk, the lepers are cleansed, and the deaf hear, the dead are raised up, the poor have the gospel preached to them." (Luke 7:20–22)

Jesus' report to John contained the proclamation of outward manifestations which showed that the Kingdom of God had come. At a future time, Jesus did announce Himself as the Lamb of God that had come to take away the sins of the world. However, His initial proclamation to John was a list of attesting miracles that proved He was the long-awaited Messiah and that the Kingdom of Heaven had indeed come to earth. After receiving the report of Jesus' reply to his servants, John was then able to die in peace, knowing the arrival of the kingdom meant the promised One had come and that his ministry was fulfilled.

John's message was also the call to repentance. From an evangelical view, we do not find the proclamation of the need for the repentance of sins to be strange. However, John's most vehement message of repentance was to the Pharisees and Sadducees, who represented the established religion of the day. This certainly was peculiar as it would not be common thought to consider the religious leaders of the day—who took great pride in keeping the law—as the ones in need of repentance. In Matthew chapter 3, many of the Pharisees and Sadducees came to John for the baptism of repentance. Knowing their hearts, John's response to them might seem harsh to many.

You brood of vipers, who warned you to flee from the wrath to come? Therefore bear fruit in keeping with repentance. (Matthew 3:7b–8)

John's message was not only one of repentance from outward sins but also of repentance from dead works and the hidden sins of the heart. The Kingdom of Heaven would not be attainable as a result of human effort or outward show but only as a free gift from the Father through the sacrifice of His Son. John is not commonly thought of as the bearer of the message of grace, but in actuality, his cry for repentance and his announcement of the coming kingdom were the precursors of grace.

Your Kingdom Come, Your Will Be Done

Jesus' teachings on the Kingdom of God give a new perspective on several familiar portions of scripture. One of these texts is 'The Lord's Prayer.' Most churchgoers were taught this prayer while they were young and may have often repeated it. Nonetheless, I know that I personally, along with many others, may have never paid attention to the reference to God's kingdom. It has only been in recent years that the Lord has revealed to me the extent and the effect—on heaven and on earth—the words in this prayer have. In Matthew's account of how Jesus told us to pray, we see the emphasis on the kingdom message.

> Pray, then, in this way: "Our Father who is in heaven, Hallowed be Your name. Your kingdom come. Your will be done, on earth as it is in heaven. Give us this day our daily bread. And forgive us our debts, as we also have forgiven our debtors. And do not lead us into temptation, but deliver us from evil. [For Yours is the kingdom, and the power, and the glory, forever. Amen.]" (Matthew 6:9–13)

We are instructed by Jesus in this model prayer to petition our Heavenly Father to send His kingdom to earth. When His kingdom comes, His will will be done on earth as it is in heaven. On the other hand, since we are the vehicles through whom His kingdom is expressed, His kingdom will not come to earth if His will is not done. More specifically, His kingdom will be experienced on earth in proportion to the extent His will is done. Expecting the literal Kingdom of Heaven to come to earth through prayer may sound radical to many Christians but is precisely what Jesus told us to pray for. Surely, He would not have instructed us to petition the Father for something He did not intend to provide.

In order to pray specifically for God's will to be done, we must know what His will is for each situation. In place of a traditional understanding of prayer—telling God our requests—there is a need for prayer to be seen as a two-way conversation with God. As we talk and commune with God during prayer, He imparts direction and insight into our spirit. I like to use the term "listening prayer," since when I pray, I anticipate having a conversation with God during which I expect Him to answer. One definition of prayer from the late Oswald Chambers is: "Prayer is telling God what I know He knows in order that I may get to know it as He does."

With this definition in mind, prayer is engaging in a two-way conversation with God in order to know His mind, feel His heart, and discern His specific will for each situation. If you are not used to listening prayer, this can seem like a slow process. However, with practice, time spent communing with God in listening prayer will give us the knowledge of His will and a progressive understanding of His ways.

Knowing God's ways also gives us a better chance of discerning His will for any given situation. Even Jesus proclaimed, "The Son can do nothing of Himself, unless it is something He sees the Father doing" (John 5:19). Jesus' commitment to only do what He saw the Father doing, which would include a commitment to only say what He heard the Father saying, gave Him the ability to continually seek and know the will of His Father. Since our spiritual gifts may not be fine-tuned to the point where we see what the Father is doing or always hear what He is saying, understanding His ways can help us know how to pray.

Releasing the Kingdom on Earth

The Lord's Prayer was given as a pattern of how we should pray. So when Jesus specifically taught us to pray for the kingdom to come and God's will to be done on earth as it is in heaven, He was showing us our responsibility as believers in releasing the Kingdom of Heaven on earth. Matthew 18:18 tells us that "whatever you bind on earth shall be bound in heaven; and whatever you loose on earth shall be loosed in heaven."

The thought of binding and loosing through prayer makes many Christians very nervous. Some do not believe this verse can be taken literally, and others fear knowing what to bind or loose. Since human nature tends to fear the unknown and shy away from the unfamiliar, this verse is largely ignored. The problem with this reaction is that we were not brought into the kingdom to retreat but were brought into the kingdom to intentionally and increasingly "occupy" (Luke 19:13, KJV) the territory that Adam and Eve forfeited to Satan—until the Lord comes. The Lord is presently seated at the right hand of the Father waiting for His body on the earth (us) to make His enemies His footstool.

> But He, having offered one sacrifice for sins for all time, sat down at the right hand of God, waiting from that time onward until his enemies be made a footstool for his feet. (Hebrews 10:12–13)

With this task at hand and in consideration of the mandate for us to bind and loose, we must refer back to the principle that God never instructs us to do anything He has not thoroughly prepared us to do. Rather than fear binding and loosing, we should be encouraged by knowing that when we speak forth God's will on earth, there will be results in the heavenly realm, which in God's timing will then be manifested on earth.

In an attempt to picture the process of releasing the Kingdom of God onto earth, I am going to use a simple illustration, which in no way is meant to be irreverent. Imagine the Kingdom of God as a department store stocked with the answers to every problem the world could ever have. There is peace, joy, love, financial provision for every material need, healthy body parts, and answers for any other person, place, or thing we would ever cry out to God for. Since the list is endless, I will let you imagine what you would ask the Lord to release from the heavenly department store onto earth.

The rules of distribution from the Kingdom Life Department Store are, first of all, the answer must be according to God's will for the situation or person we are praying for, and secondly, the release of the answer must be according to God's timing. God's will and God's timing are both important keys to remember as we train to release the Kingdom of God on earth through prayer.

In regards to the timing of the Lord, Father once spoke to my heart (with a smile), "You speak forth the things I give you and I will schedule them." In other words, it is our job to faithfully proclaim what the Lord shows us, when He shows us. God, however, brings forth His will in the "fullness of times" (Ephesians 1:10, KJV). The fullness of times can be compared to the development of a baby in a mother's womb. If the baby is born prematurely—at best—it will struggle to live. In the worse scenario, the baby may have permanent defects or die. Similarly, only God knows when all that He has worked behind the scenes is "full-term" and ready to be released onto the earth. Since God's ways and thoughts are so much higher than ours, His answers often do not look as we expected and often come after a much longer wait than we would have chosen. Scripture and countless believers, however, testify to the fact that those who wait on the Lord will never be disappointed.

> For from days of old they have not heard or perceived by ear, nor has the eye seen a God besides You, Who acts in behalf of the one who waits for Him. (Isaiah 64:4)

> Now to Him who is able to do far more abundantly beyond all that we ask or think, according to the power that works within us. (Ephesians 3:20)

God is the only one Who sees the beginning from the end, and only He knows when our answer is ready to be delivered. For this reason, we must do our best to accurately speak forth what we perceive God is saying—even when we may not understand the big picture. At the same time, we must not allow fear to cause us to draw back and fail to release what God has revealed to us. Just continue to remember that God is in control. He is aware of the frailty of our flesh even more so than we are. He knows the motive of our hearts and our desire—or lack of it—to be faithful servants. In all things, we can rest in His love, depend on His grace, and trust Him to express His will on the earth through yielded vessels—no matter how flawed.

The mandate of releasing God's kingdom onto earth through prayer is of far more consequence than being concerned about our performance record. What we really need to be concerned with is not praying—no matter what excuses we may come up with. If we do not pray, most often God's will will not be done on earth. Scripture does not teach that God will never move on earth apart from the petitions of His people, but scripture is clear that prayer is certainly the normal method God uses to release His will on earth, as it is in heaven.

Our First Priority Must Be His Kingdom

God's kingdom department store is available to meet the needs of not only His children but also the needs of those around us He desires to touch. The Kingdom of God is surely at hand, and Matthew chapter 6 teaches us the priority of seeking His kingdom.

> But seek first His kingdom and His righteousness; and all these things shall be added to you. (Matthew 6:33)

This is a common scripture. Nonetheless, let us think for a moment as to how His kingdom is sought and how His righteousness is obtained. Depending on our background, each one of us might have a slightly different perspective as to how the Kingdom of God is to be pursued. Many would likely associate some form of Christian discipline as the method of seeking the kingdom, but scripture is clear that "by the works of the Law no flesh will be justified" (Romans 3:20). The Kingdom of God and the righteousness of God are personified in Christ Jesus and become ours through faith. Even as our growth in the kingdom continues, it will always be faith through grace that compels us to seek His kingdom and His righteousness above all else.

We need to ask our Heavenly Father to open our spiritual eyes to see and understand what the Kingdom of God on earth really is. In the tenth chapter of Matthew, Jesus began to teach His disciples what the kingdom on earth would look like. This verse can be seen as a vital part of the mission statement for His body, the church.

> And as you go, preach, saying, "The Kingdom of Heaven is at hand." Heal the sick, raise the dead, cleanse the lepers, cast out demons. Freely you received, freely give. (Matthew 10:7–8)

Jesus was clearly instructing His disciples that what they were being sent forth to do was to proclaim that the Kingdom of God had come. We know that at the time Jesus was teaching them, the disciples did not understand the depth of what they were to proclaim. Due to their Jewish background, they still believed Jesus was going to set up a physical kingdom on earth, which would free them from the tyranny of the Roman government. Although they saw the power and manifestations of the kingdom in the life and ministry of Jesus Christ, their preconceived mental image of what they wanted the kingdom to be caused them to miss the reality of what Jesus taught.

Even the apostles who lived and ministered with Jesus did not fully understand the reality of the kingdom they were proclaiming. In the same way, it is likely the majority of the modern-day church does not understand how the Kingdom of God is to be experienced on this earth. No particular camp in the body of Christ has a corner on understanding the kingdom. However, the revelation of kingdom life has been received by a remnant among many denominations and nondenominations that make up His body.

The Kingdom Is Within Us

When the apostle Peter stated, "His divine power has granted to us everything pertaining to life and godliness" (2 Peter 1:3), he meant everything! All we need for life and godliness—His divine power— is already available to us while we live on this earth, as citizens of heaven. The divine life of Christ in our hearts not only gives us the fruit of the Spirit but also every gift, office, and ministration of the Spirit, every attribute of His nature, all the blessings of Abraham, and the Father's favor toward His Son—all as our own. The Kingdom of

God really is within us! All that we could ever imagine Jesus being or having available to Him is available to us because He is our life. His nature and all it stands for was exchanged for our nature at the time of new birth.

The nature of someone or something determines how it thinks, feels, and acts. When we act according to our new nature, we will act like Jesus. Jesus was the incarnate Kingdom of Heaven on earth. Since the Kingdom of God is a spiritual realm, there had to be a fleshly channel through which the Spirit of God could be expressed to mankind. Jesus brought the Kingdom of Heaven to earth by humbling Himself and becoming a man. In the words of the late Sir Ian Thomas, we should be "the visible image of the invisible God." Since it is impossible for true manifestations of the kingdom to come forth from the self-effort of mankind, demonstrations of the kingdom can only come from the release of the divine nature of Christ, abiding in us.

The Kingdom of God will also displace the Kingdom of Darkness to the extent we allow Jesus to live His life through us. Our everyday acquaintances will be drawn to Jesus to the extent they are touched by the Kingdom of Heaven while in our presence. Jesus said, "And I, if I be lifted up from the earth, will draw all men to Myself" (John 12:32).

Since apart from the treasure within us we are only earthen vessels, those around us will be drawn to Jesus during the times we allow the Holy Spirit to rule over our flesh. Each and every day we are given the opportunity to walk after the flesh (represented by the Tree of the Knowledge of Good and Evil) or after the spirit (represented by the Tree of Life).

For the believer, the Adamic nature was crucified with Christ, but the flesh, which is the part of our mind, will, and emotions that was trained by our old nature, is earthly, sensual, and prone to demonic influence. Jesus took our old nature to the cross with Him to set us free from the power of sin. When we are born again, we can still choose to sin, but we no longer have to. As we choose to yield to the spirit, rather than to the flesh, the Kingdom of God will be seen and experienced.

Jesus brought the Kingdom of Heaven to earth. While He walked this earth in bodily form, the kingdom was seen in His life. He then took us to the cross with Him (Romans 6:1–14) in order to exchange His nature for our nature. Through this exchange, Christ is still present in bodily form, but His presence is expressed through a multi-membered or corporate body.

In reality, all we could ever conceive with our finite minds that Jesus could make available to us is included in the phrase "the Kingdom of God." As we will see in succeeding chapters, the Kingdom of God contains more than we could ever imagine!

What Is the Problem?

A word that is commonly used when the unseen is perceived with at least one of our five senses is "manifest." With this definition in mind, why is there very little manifestation of the Kingdom of God on earth? Why are people and places not touched by the kingdom? Why has the presence of the Kingdom of Heaven on the earth for over 2,000 years made very little change in the status quo?

The problem is threefold. First, few believers have a biblical understanding of the Kingdom of Heaven—"My people are destroyed for lack of knowledge" (Hosea 4:6). We must know the truth about the kingdom to such an extent that the unseen becomes more real to us than the seen.

The second reason is lack of faith in the word of God. Knowledge in itself will not release the kingdom into our lives. We must meditate on the word of the Lord until it produces the faith to walk in an unseen kingdom: "Now faith is the substance of things hoped for, the evidence of things not seen" (Hebrews 11:1, NKJV).

The last reason is an issue of choice. Even when we know the truth and have the faith that what we know is true beyond a shadow of a doubt, we still must choose to yield to the truth by acting upon it. Making daily choices as an act of our will, based on the truth of God's word, regardless of how we feel or what things look like, is vital for victory in our Christian walk.

One Last Word

All the ushering in of the Kingdom of Heaven entails became available to you and I through Jesus Christ. The text we began this chapter with from the gospel of Mark proclaims Jesus' purpose for coming to earth: "The time is fulfilled, and the Kingdom of God is at hand; repent and believe in the Gospel."

We in the body of Christ must repent from the practice of preaching the part of the kingdom message that each of us are most fond of. In order to repent, we must change our ways and preach all the bible declares in regards to the kingdom. Evangelicals proudly say 'we preach Jesus' with an inference that 'kingdom talk' might 'clutter' "the simplicity and purity of devotion to Christ" (2 Corinthians 11:3). When in reality, the bible clearly teaches if we preach about Jesus we are proclaiming the Kingdom of God—Jesus was the incarnation of the kingdom!

Our lack of understanding of the kingdom and/or willingness to proclaim it is the equivalent to the scrolls of the law in Josiah's time being buried under layers of dust. The layers of dust of neglect, tradition, preset ideas, apathy, and spiritual blindness have covered the truth of the Kingdom of God that is needed to set the captives free. In order to be like our Savior, we too must proclaim: "Repent for the Kingdom of Heaven is at hand" (Matthew 4:17b)!

CHAPTER 2

Only the Righteous Will Enter

The title to this chapter would be enough to cause many of us to give up on the hope of kingdom life. If only the righteous will enter the Kingdom of God, then the excitement stirred from the first chapter just fizzled. Most of us are honest enough to admit that no matter how hard we try to follow in the steps of our Savior, we fall short of righteousness. Just in case you happen to believe you are righteous in comparison to others you know, remember God's standard of righteousness is Christ. Next to a Holy God, "All our righteous deeds are like a filthy garment" (Isaiah 64:6).

In the fifth chapter of Matthew, Jesus made an amazing statement.

Do not think that I came to abolish the Law or the Prophets; I did not come to abolish, but to fulfill. For truly I say to you, until heaven and earth pass away, not the smallest letter or stroke shall pass away from the Law, until all is accomplished. Whoever then annuls one of the least of these commandments, and so teaches others, shall be called least in the Kingdom of Heaven; but whoever keeps and teaches them, he shall be called great in the Kingdom of Heaven. For I say unto you, that unless your righteousness surpasses that of the scribes and Pharisees, you shall not enter the Kingdom of Heaven. You have heard that the ancients were told, "YOU SHALL NOT COMMIT MURDER" and "Whoever commits murder shall be liable to the court." But I say to you that everyone who is angry with his brother shall be guilty before the court; and whoever shall say to his brother, "Raca,"* shall be guilty enough to go into the fiery hell. (Matthew 5:17–22)

*Raca: An Aramaic word of utter contempt that signifies empty—intellectually rather than moral. In other words, "empty-headed." Worse than just anger—for at least anger in itself is contained within—Raca would be an outward expression of the inward anger.

Jesus was speaking to Jews who understood that the life goal of the scribes and Pharisees was to analyze, debate, and keep the law. Their whole self-worth was dependent on their accomplishment of this purpose. If there were segments of the population who were considered righteous, it was certainly the scribes and Pharisees.

To further stress the point, if scribes or Pharisees were able to keep the law—which was measured by outward appearance—they would have considered themselves successful in their life goal of attaining godliness. In other words, if you were a scribe or Pharisee, the only achievement in life worth attaining was the keeping of the law.

The audience Jesus addressed in Matthew 5:20 included scribes and Pharisees. Jesus purposely used them as an example of self-effort, as opposed to the age of grace He was ushering in. For that reason, when He stated that "unless your righteousness surpasses that of the scribes and Pharisees, you shall not enter the Kingdom of Heaven," He declared war on the religious system of His time.

The common people in the crowd who heard Jesus' words certainly could have lost all hope of entering the Kingdom of Heaven. They, of all people, knew that if the scribes and Pharisees—whose sole purpose for living was the keeping of the law—were not righteous enough to enter the kingdom, then certainly they would not be able to enter either.

Motives of the Heart

Jesus laid out His defense by quoting the law in regards to murder and then likened murder to anger! To his listeners, there was no comparison. He began this train of thought by saying if they were angry with their brother they were guilty before the court. He then progressed to say if they called their brother "empty-headed," they would be guilty before the Supreme Court. He climaxed this contrast to murder with the statement that if they called their brother a fool—which would be comparable to a godless, moral reprobate—they would be guilty of hell.

Jesus was teaching them by this series of examples that there was no way they could possibly achieve righteousness in their own strength. He went from declaring their righteousness would have to exceed that of the scribes and Pharisees to teaching that rather than their outward acts, what God was really interested in was the attitudes of their hearts. Even if they were able to keep every bit of the law, which governed every visible aspect of life, they knew what was in their hearts would keep them from gaining entrance to the Kingdom of Heaven.

In verse 21, Jesus quoted from Exodus 20:13, where the Ten Commandments were given to the people of Israel. Jesus stated the obvious—that they should not commit murder—but then began to teach about His kingdom. In verse 22, He explained the guilt the attitude behind their words would place upon them. In the Kingdom of God, the condition and motive of their hearts is what they would be held accountable to.

Performance-Based Acceptance

To apply this teaching to our day and age, just think of the number of religious groups who do not believe the finished work of Jesus Christ is the only basis for salvation. These groups are trying to make themselves acceptable to God based on what they can do. Not only is this an impossible task, but it leads to hypocrisy and burnout.

In those who are not honest enough to admit the areas they fall short in, hypocrisy is bred as they try to conceal the secrets of their hearts. Moreover, on the other side of self-righteousness are those honest enough to acknowledge they cannot please God and give up trying to achieve an impossible task.

The sad thing about those who try to make themselves acceptable to God by what they do or do not do is that this group is not exclusively made up of unbelievers. A large portion of the body of Christ still lives as though they believe they are not acceptable to God unless they keep the list of 'dos and don'ts' they personally embrace. Although they may give mental assent to God's total acceptance of them by grace through faith, deep down in their hearts they do not feel accepted by God the Father. The motives of their hearts and their imperfect performance condemn them.

Receive Righteousness as a Gift or Do Without

In order to walk in the kingdom, we must know there is nothing we can do to produce righteousness. Furthermore, any righteousness we have is a result of the "gift" of our Heavenly Father through faith in our Lord Jesus Christ. The late Oswald Chambers was dedicated to the body of Christ's understanding of this truth. In the November 28 entry of his classic devotional, *My Utmost for His Highest*, he stated, "We have to realize that we cannot earn or win anything from God; we must either receive it as a gift or do without it."

> But now apart from the Law the righteousness of God has been manifested, being witnessed by the Law and the Prophets, even the righteousness of God through faith in Jesus Christ for all those who believe; for there is no distinction; for all have sinned and fall short of the glory of God, being justified as a gift by His grace through the redemption which is in Christ Jesus. (Romans 3:21–24)

> But when the kindness of God our Savior and His love for mankind appeared, He saved us, not on the basis of deeds which we have done in righteousness, but according to His mercy, by the washing of regeneration and renewing by the Holy Spirit,

whom He poured out upon us richly through Jesus Christ our Savior, so that being justified by His grace we would be made heirs according to the hope of eternal life. (Titus 3:4–7)

Actually, scripture is very clear in declaring our imputed righteousness from faith in Jesus Christ alone. The problem is, our mortal minds cannot understand how this can be, so we continue to look to our own righteousness even as the scribes and Pharisees did. We live our lives either puffed up when we are able to keep our list of 'dos and don'ts' or condemned when we fail. Either of these ditches along the narrow path is destructive.

The crowds of Jews that initially followed Jesus knew only of the law and had no idea how righteousness could ever be imputed. After one of the occasions on which Jesus supernaturally fed the multitude of people that had come to listen to His teaching, He was asked this question:

Therefore they said to Him, "What shall we do, so that we may work the works of God?" Jesus answered and said to them, "This is the work of God, that you believe in Him whom He has sent." (John 6:28–29)

The bible also tells us:

Brethren, my heart's desire and my prayer to God for them is for their salvation. For I testify about them that they have a zeal for God, but not in accordance with knowledge. For not knowing about God's righteousness and seeking to establish their own, they did not subject themselves to the righteousness of God. For Christ is the end of the law for righteousness to everyone who believes. (Romans 10:1–5)

That if you confess with your mouth Jesus as Lord, and believe in your heart that God raised Him from the dead, you will be saved; for with the heart a person believes, resulting in righteousness, and with the mouth he confesses, resulting in salvation. (Romans 10:9–10)

Responses to a Holy God

As it is hard to grasp the fact that God's righteousness instantly becomes ours as a result of believing on the Lord Jesus Christ, mankind has had an inclination to respond to a holy God in three ways.

Our first tendency is to work to earn God's approval according to what we think His expectations are—in an attempt to please Him. The problem is, if we are looking to our own good works to please God, we will never measure up. This will leave us prone to feeling unloved and unaccepted by our Heavenly Father. These negative emotions place us on a never-ending performance treadmill. Regretfully, many on the performance treadmill finally wear out, leave the faith, and renounce Christianity as something that did not work for them.

When we do not understand that our righteousness is in Christ alone, the next way we can respond to God is to focus on our own good works rather than on Jesus. Since we think there must be something we can do to please God, we relive and reiterate what we consider to be our good works in order to feel righteous in God's eyes and holy before our particular "religious" community. However, God knew if there was anything we could do to make ourselves righteous or to earn His favor, that we would brag about it.

> For by grace you have been saved through faith; and that not of yourselves, it is the gift of God; not as a result of works, that no one should boast. (Ephesians 2:8–9)

Since this is our tendency, God made it very clear in His word that there is absolutely nothing we can do in our own strength (from our flesh) that can be counted as righteousness toward our 'accepted-by-God' account. Scripture is also very clear in its teaching that when we strive to be holy through self-effort—self-effort being the application of our own law—we will actually obtain the opposite results from those desired.

> For the Law brings about wrath, but where there is no law, there also is no violation. (Romans 4:15)

The law truly does bring about "wrath." The Greek word translated as "wrath" in this verse is *"orgē." Strong's Exhaustive Concordance of the Bible* defines *orgē* as "desire (as a reaching forth or excitement of the mind)," such as "violent passion." The usage in Romans 4:15 is the thought that when law is applied to any situation, it brings about a strong passion in our flesh for the very thing the law opposes. Whatever we try to do to be righteous before God is the "law" that we put ourselves under and the result of the law is a fleshly attempt toward righteousness—no matter how religious it is or how good it looks.

The late A. B. Simpson wrote, "As long as we struggle under law—that is, by our own effort—sin shall have dominion over us. But the moment we step from under the shadow of Sinai and throw ourselves upon the simple grace of Christ and His free and absolute gift of righteousness, the struggle is practically over."[2]

The third response from striving for a righteousness of our own is pride. Pride builds itself up by condemning those around us who do not measure up to our manual on "holy living." It also often results in harsh attitudes and intolerance toward those who have not measured up to our standards. Pride further wounds those in the body of Christ who are already feeling unworthy of Christ's love and then feel like hopeless failures in light of others' glowing performance-based accounts.

The Great Exchange

Until we can rest in the fact that Jesus' death made a way for us to obtain His righteousness, we will continue to seek a righteousness

---

[2.] *Days of Heaven on Earth*, A. B. Simpson, March 17

of our own. Even if only subconscious, this mind-set will rob us of abundant life, which is kingdom life.

> Therefore if anyone is in Christ, he is a new creature; the old things passed away; behold, new things have come. Now all these things are from God, who reconciled us to Himself through Christ and gave us the ministry of reconciliation, namely, that God was in Christ reconciling the world to Himself, not counting their trespasses against them, and He has committed to us the word of reconciliation. Therefore, we are ambassadors for Christ, as though God were making an appeal through us; we beg you on behalf of Christ, be reconciled to God. He made Him who knew no sin to be sin on our behalf, that we might become the righteousness of God in Him. (2 Corinthians 5:17–21)

Although it is true evangelical Christianity typically recognizes the importance of 2 Corinthians 5:17, it is commonly taught that we are responsible to make "the old things" pass away and make the "new things" come. Instead of being taught that the natural flow of being "in Christ" will make our lives a reflection of Him, we are taught performance modification—whether directly or by inference.

The Amplified Bible inserts—after the word being defined—the meaning of the original text in parenthesis. The Amplified Bible's translation of 2 Corinthians 5:17 gives a very accurate rendering and is worthy of examination.

> Therefore if any person is [ingrafted] in Christ [the Messiah] he is a new creation [a new creature altogether]; the old [previous moral and spiritual condition] has passed away. Behold, the fresh and new has come! (2 Corinthians 5:17, AMPC)

Since we were originally born into Adam's family tree, we had to somehow get out of Adam's bloodline. If we could trace our family heritage back to Adam, we would find that all of us have Adam as our great-great-great-grandfather. When we were born again, we were "[ingrafted] in Christ" (see also Romans 11:17–24). Our adoption as sons by our Heavenly Father—through faith in Jesus Christ (Galatians 4:4–6)—removed us from Adam's family tree and placed us in the family of God.

Not only were we grafted into the family tree of the Lord, but we became "a new creature altogether" through the exchange of our old sinful nature for the nature of Christ. The old "previous moral and spiritual condition" of our inner man is gone, and we have become a new creation.

Jesus Christ bore our sinful nature on the cross, and He gives His righteous nature as an even exchange to all who believe on Him. When God the Father—Who is spirit—looks at us, He looks at our spirit-man and sees the righteous nature of His Son. As long as we are united with Christ, we are unconditionally righteous. Our righteousness has absolutely nothing to do with our performance. To the believer in Christ, sin has nothing to do with righteousness (see Appendix I, "Confession of Sin").

> For Christ did not enter a holy place made with hands, a mere copy of the true one, but into heaven itself, now to appear in the presence of God for us; nor was it that He would offer Himself often, as the high priest enters the holy place year by year with blood that is not his own. Otherwise, He would have needed to suffer often since the foundation of the world; but now once at the consummation of the ages He has been manifested to put away sin by the sacrifice of Himself. And inasmuch as it is appointed for men to die once and after this comes judgment, so Christ also, having been offered once to bear the sins of many, will appear a second time for salvation without reference to sin, to those who eagerly await Him. (Hebrews 9:24–28)

According to *Strong's Hebrew and Greek Dictionaries*, the words "put away" are a translation of the Greek word "*athetēsis.*" This word means "cancellation," which in this text is the cancellation of sin. This cancellation of sin is not just the sin we have asked forgiveness for but for all of our sin—past, present, and future. All sin was canceled through the one-time sacrifice of Jesus Christ for the sin of mankind.

When we accepted Jesus as our Savior, His righteousness was applied to us. For this reason, when He appears on the earth the "second time," it will be "without reference to sin." This is possible because He is our atoning sacrifice or our propitiation. The word "propitiation" is Latin and brings into its English translation the connotation of "heathen rites for winning the favor, or averting the anger, of the gods" (*International Standard Bible Encyclopedia*). The NASB side reference defines propitiation as "satisfaction." If we are born again, God the Father is judicially/completely satisfied with us.

There is a working out of our salvation—a work of the Spirit of Sanctification—resulting in holiness as we begin to walk after the spirit rather than after the flesh. We walk out our grace-enabled destiny of being conformed to the image of Christ. However, none of the deeper works of the Holy Spirit in our lives have anything to do with our righteousness (right standing before God). This is not too good to be true. This is the truth!

> You know that He appeared in order to take away sins; and in Him there is no sin. (1 John 3:5)

Another witness to this truth comes from 1 John 3. There, Jesus appeared to "take away" our sins. "Take away" is translated from the Greek word *"airō."* According to *The Expanded Vines Expository Dictionary of New Testament Words*, the meaning of *"airō"* in this verse is the same meaning given in John 1:29.

> The next day he saw Jesus coming to him and said, "Behold, the Lamb of God who takes away the sin of the world!" (John 1:29)

In both verses, the phrase "take away" is used to depict Christ taking away the sin of the world (not individual sins but sin). The *Vine's Dictionary* describes this as "that which has existed from the time of the Fall, and in regard to which God has had judicial dealings with the world; through the expiatory sacrifice of Christ the sin of the world will be replaced by everlasting righteousness." Christ not only came to take away our sins (verb), but just as important, He replaced our inherent sinfulness with His righteousness.

> Seeing that His divine power has given us all things that are needful for life and godliness, through our knowledge of Him who has appealed to us by His own glorious perfections. It is by means of these that He has granted us His precious and wondrous promises, in order that through them you may, one and all, become sharers in the very nature of God, having completely escaped the corruption which exists in the world through earthly cravings. (2 Peter 1:3–4, 1912 Weymouth New Testament)

We received the "very nature of God" upon new birth. The nature of something or someone determines how it or they will act or think. We would have no hope of Christlikeness without His nature within us. As we apply the truth of our new nature to our lives by faith, we will begin to experience the outworking of His life. The power of His endless life gives "us all things that are needful for life and godliness." Our experience of the Kingdom of God will increase as a result of the imputed righteousness of Christ permeating every segment of our lives.

Grace-Enabled Growth

All that we have in the Lord is a gift from our Heavenly Father. Apart from the drawing of the Holy Spirit, we would not even have had the ability to accept Christ's gift of salvation. As we begin to know God's ways, we realize every step of our continued growth in Christ is through the power of His grace.

> But by His doing you are in Christ Jesus, who became to us wisdom from God, and righteousness and sanctification, and redemption. (1 Corinthians 1:30)

But it is from Him that you have your life in Christ Jesus, Whom God made our Wisdom from God, [revealed to us a knowledge of the divine plan of salvation previously hidden, manifesting itself as] our Righteousness [thus making us upright and putting us in right standing with God], and our Consecration [making us pure and holy], and our Redemption [providing our ransom from the eternal penalty for sin]. (1 Corinthians 1:30, AMPC)

Through Christ, the Father brought us into His family and "revealed to us a knowledge of the divine plan of salvation" through His 'Word' (Hebrews 4:12, AMPC). This is in reference to both the impartation of Christ's life (the Word) within us and the teaching regarding Christ in the written Word.

We had, and still have, no righteousness of our own. In order for us to have fellowship with our Heavenly Father, He made provision for us to be made righteous apart from our performance.

God's Word tells us to be holy, even as He is holy. In the face of this impossibility, God provided the means for the outworking of holiness in our lives. He gave us the gift of the divine nature in our innermost being, placed His Spirit within us, and floods us with His grace.

Our Father then finished the package (the gift) by redeeming us and "providing our ransom from" the "eternal penalty for sin" through the once-for-all sacrifice of His Son. Only the righteous will enter the kingdom, but God the Father Himself made the provision for this righteousness through our Lord Jesus Christ.

Our emphasis in this book is not how to enter the Kingdom of God but how to walk in and experience an invisible kingdom while living on this earth. The only way to experience the fruit and power of the Kingdom of Heaven is by embracing Christ's righteousness as a gift and by resting in His finished work on the cross.

CHAPTER 3

The Violent Take It by Force

So far in our search for the Kingdom of God, we have discovered that the kingdom exists on this earth—here and now. The kingdom is a spiritual kingdom, and it is God's intent for His kingdom to be manifested in the lives of its citizens. Salvation isn't taken by force, but the kingdom is!

The concept of force being necessary to take a spiritual kingdom is so foreign to human thought that Paul and Barnabus, while on their missionary journeys, went to great lengths to encourage the brethren in regards to tribulations to come.

> Strengthening the souls of the disciples, encouraging them to continue in the faith, and saying, "Through many tribulations we must enter the Kingdom of God." (Acts 14:22)

Several of the meanings for the word from which "tribulations" is derived give us a vivid picture of what we should expect as we walk in an unseen kingdom in a contrary world—"pressure, affliction, anguish, and persecution."[3]

The disciples knew the assault against the Kingdom of God spreading around the world would be so intense believers would

---

[3.] Strong's Hebrew and Greek Dictionaries, e-sword

need to know the cost of experiencing the kingdom on earth before they faced the fury of the opposition.

> Whoever does not carry his own cross and come after Me cannot be My disciple. For which one of you, when he wants to build a tower, does not first sit down and calculate the cost to see if he has enough to complete it? (Luke 14:27–28)

> Or what king, when he sets out to meet another king in battle, will not first sit down and consider whether he is strong enough with ten thousand men to encounter the one coming against him with twenty thousand? Or else, while the other is still far away, he sends a delegation and asks for terms of peace. (Luke 14:31–32)

We Work Out Our Salvation

This leads us to a very important key to kingdom living: "violent men take it by force" (Matthew 11:12b). This could seem contradictory because in the last chapter we saw very explicitly that nothing we can do can make us worthy of the kingdom. Our imputed righteousness and new nature are free gifts, but the working out of what was placed inside us at new birth requires perseverance!

> So then, my beloved, just as you have always obeyed, not as in my presence only, but now much more in my absence, work out your salvation with fear and trembling. (Philippians 2:12)

The "working out of our salvation" seems contradictory to the grace of God, but we need to consider this concept within the framework of the whole counsel of God. In fact, Philippians 2:13 looks as if it is in direct conflict with verse 12 quoted above.

> For it is God who is at work in you, both to will and to work for His good pleasure. (Philippians 2:13)

39

Through our obedience to the known will of God, we work out our salvation. Yet, at the same time, it is God Who gives us the power to obey. Not only does our Lord give us the power to obey, but He also gives us the desire to obey. In light of this, what part of the "working out of our salvation" is God doing and what part is up to us?

God gave us our own freewill because He wants us to obey Him out of love and not out of compulsion. At the same time—as our Creator—He knows the frailty of our flesh and gave us all we need for life and godliness through the implantation of His divine nature at new birth. Our part then is to acknowledge our desperate need for the grace of God to enable us to be obedient children—His ability for our inability. His response to the acknowledgment of our need is to pour out His grace upon us. In the times when we do not want to yield to the Holy Spirit, God will even give us the desire to do His will—if we will only ask.

A Violent Passion to Walk in His Ways

With the realization there is nothing we can do in our own strength, we must still want all that God has for us—more than our next breath. This passion to walk in His ways is what the scripture calls "violent."

> Truly, I say to you, among those born of women there has not arisen anyone greater than John the Baptist; yet he who is least in the Kingdom of Heaven is greater than he. And from the days of John the Baptist until now the Kingdom of Heaven suffers violence, and violent men take it by force. (Matthew 11:11–12)

In order to understand the use of the word "violent" in reference to experiencing the Kingdom of God, we can look to the example of the Israelites in the Old Testament. The nation of Israel, when in bondage to Egypt, serves as a type or an example of a person before they accept Christ. We were all citizens of the Kingdom of

Darkness (Egypt), and our spiritual father was the devil—no matter how good we were. We are in either the Kingdom of Darkness or in the Kingdom of Light. There is no in-between.

When the nation of Israel crossed the Red Sea, it was a picture of our being delivered from the Kingdom of Darkness to the Kingdom of God's Dear Son. The Promised Land or Canaan is synonymous with abundant life or kingdom life. Regretfully, the majority of God's children will live and die in the wilderness without ever entering the Promised Land. God's intention has always been for us to experience His kingdom on earth, rather than for us to die in the 'Wilderness of Sin.'

The consensus of bible scholars is that Canaan was only seven to eleven days from the Red Sea, and yet the children of Israel never entered the land. Why were they not allowed to enter? The third chapter of Hebrews gives us a clear answer.

> And so we see that they were not able to enter because of unbelief. (Hebrews 3:19)

They did not enter the land of abundance God had ordained for them, because they would not believe what God promised was possible when what they could see with their mortal eyes spoke to the contrary. The definition of faith extracted from Hebrews 11:1 is, "believing in something you cannot see and acting upon it as if you could." Since the Israelites could not imagine how they could overcome the giants and the walled cities in the land, they refused to believe what God said He would do. This unbelief cost them their inheritance.

As we continue to study the Kingdom of Heaven in the chapters yet to come, we will see the spiritual riches that comprise the counterpart of the Promised Land—the land that flowed with milk and honey. We, too, will only experience the abundant life that Canaan represents to the extent we believe we can have abundant life in our lives on this earth. Our Heavenly Father will purposely allow 'giants' in our lives to taunt us—to see how serious we are about taking possession of the "land of promise" (Hebrews 11:9). We must believe that what God says is more real than what our five senses tell us!

In the biblical account of taking the land, the Israelites were guaranteed the victory but still had to conquer each city. The literal cities represent trials in our lives or the strongholds in our flesh we must overcome to experience kingdom life. In the case of the cities in Canaan, some were conquered by methods of war we would consider quite normal, and some were supernaturally given to the children of Israel. The same holds true for us as we press into God's grace to overcome the 'cities' in our lives. We will be delivered instantly from some strongholds of our flesh, and yet other trials will seem to go on forever—seemingly unnoticed by our Heavenly Father. What is important to remember is that God's people were only victorious when they obeyed His every command to the last detail. In order to experience kingdom life, we must determine in our hearts that by the grace of God we will uncompromisingly obey His revealed will for our lives.

The tragedy in the example of the Israelites is that they spent the rest of their existence on this earth wandering around in circles in the wilderness. Instead of partaking of huge clusters of grapes, milk, and honey, they lived on the same manna day in and day out. For the rest of their lives, they lived on manna only intended to sustain them for seven to eleven days as they journeyed through the wilderness. Eventually, they whined until God gave them meat in the form of quails, but the meat came with God's judgment for their ingratitude. The manna was given as a short-term provision, and the quails were God's response to the Israelite's complaining. They were His good measure but not His best. What He had planned and desired for them was abundance.

This is where the majority of Christians are today. They are in the Kingdom of Light and have been set free from the Kingdom of Darkness. Yet, their everyday lives are not much different in quality than the unbelievers around them. Their Christian experience is the equivalent of the same old manna day in and day out because they have not chosen to enter the Promised Land. Battles must be won to enter the land, and this requires absolute obedience to and complete dependence on God. When the going gets tough, it is easier to give into the lies of the enemy and choose to live in mediocrity instead of fighting "the good fight of faith" (1 Timothy 6:12). We must have an unwavering commitment to fight for God's best if we are to experience the Kingdom of Heaven on earth.

According to the *Vine's Expository Dictionary*, the Greek word for violent is *"biastes."* The meaning of this word is very literal, "a forceful or violent man." Matthew 11:12 is a very literal translation. The Kingdom of Heaven will be taken or experienced by forceful, violent men (no gender intended). In order to walk in kingdom life, you will have to be forceful in the fight against your flesh and against the powers of darkness or you will not prevail—few will enter the land.

The life of Christ within us gives us all the power we need to be victorious. However, both our flesh and Satan are clever foes. In order to overcome, we must "abhor what is evil; cling to what is good" (Romans 12:9). There are times when the battle is so strong that we feel like we are going crazy or that our insides are about to explode. During these times of testing, we must cling to the Word of God.

"Faith comes by hearing, and hearing by the word of Christ" (Romans 10:17). If we do not have the word of the Lord to stand on in a particular battle, we have no basis for real faith. Since it is inevitable that we will experience intense struggles in this life, we will only overcome if we have unwavering faith in the power of God to bring to pass what He has said.

> But thanks be to God, Who always leads us in His triumph in Christ, and manifests through us the sweet aroma of the knowledge of Him in every place. (2 Corinthians 2:14)

If we really believe what the Word of God teaches about the Kingdom of Heaven, we will let nothing stop us until we experience the abundant life that awaits us.

> Violent men seize it by force [as a precious prize]—a share in the heavenly kingdom is sought for with most ardent zeal and intense exertion. (Matthew 11:12b, AMPC)

The apostle Paul obviously understood the value of the kingdom when he exclaimed, "I press on toward the goal for the prize of the upward call of God in Christ Jesus" (Philippians 3:14). He understood that there was nothing more important in life than the upward call of God. When we think of "call," we have a tendency to think of the ministry or occupation God has ordained for us. However, the apostle Paul understood that when Christ became his life, his occupation from that day on was to allow Christ to rule and reign in his heart. When Christ rules in our heart, the Kingdom of God is allowed to come forth. Paul's heart-cry in Philippians 3:14 is in reality the same admonition recorded in Matthew 6:33.

> But seek first the kingdom and His righteousness; and all these things shall be added to you. (Matthew 6:33)

In contrast to seeking the Kingdom of God with "ardent zeal and intense exertion," most of us whine if we have to stretch our spiritual muscles much at all. Regretfully, the pampered American lifestyle has not fostered the steadfastness, determination, and character necessary to possess the land.

There are two pictures that come to mind when I think of pressing toward the mark as if nothing else matters. The first picture is a crowd of children at an Easter egg hunt. The kids are all lined up along a rope, with the rope being the only thing restraining them. When the whistle is blown, they charge onto the field with no thought of anything or anyone else around them other than being the first to reach the special eggs.

On the adult scale, I can picture a group of adults outside the doors of a ticket office where a limited amount of tickets for a sports event or concert are about to be offered. When the doors open, the rush of the mob could be life-threatening.

Yet, we as Christians have the "pearl of great value" (Matthew 13:46) offered to us and are not willing to give all in order to obtain such a priceless reward. We obviously do not understand what we are missing when we fail to seek the Kingdom of God above all else.

According to *Matthew Henry's Bible Commentary*, the intent of the original language of the word "violent" found in Matthew 11:12 can be expressed, "strive to enter; a holy violence; we must run, wrestle, fight, be in agony; and we must overcome 'opposition from without and within.'"

Our Flesh—the Battle from Within

The expression in the original language for "violent" that may be the easiest to illustrate is the last on Matthew Henry's list: "we must overcome 'opposition from without and within.'" The opposition from within that we must wrestle is our flesh. (Remember that our old nature was crucified with Christ, but there still is that portion of our mind, will, and emotions that was programmed by our old nature. Imagine this as the 'ghost of the old man.')

> For the flesh sets its desire against the Spirit, and the Spirit against the flesh; for these are in opposition to one another, so that you may not do the things that you please. (Galatians 5:17)

This 'tug-of-war' between the flesh and the spirit is the opposition from within. When we choose—as an act of our will—to do the revealed will of God in our lives, the unrenewed part of us (flesh) will try to demand that we listen to what it wants. The prompting of our flesh can range from a slight nag to a raging inferno. This battle is not always easy. In order to enjoy the fruit of the Spirit that is ours as we walk in the kingdom, we will need to possess "a holy violence." The account of Christ in the Garden of Gethsemane gives us a vivid illustration of the battle between the flesh and the spirit.

> And they came to a place named Gethsemane; and He said to His disciples, "Sit here until I have prayed." And He took with Him Peter and James and John, and began to be very distressed and troubled. And He said to them, "My soul is deeply grieved to the point of death; remain here and keep watch." And He went a little beyond them, and fell to the ground, and began

to pray that if it were possible, the hour might pass Him by. And He was saying, "Abba! Father! All things are possible for You; remove this cup from Me; yet not what I will, but what You will." And He came and found them sleeping, and said to Peter, "Simon, are you asleep? Could you not keep watch for one hour?" Keep watching and praying, that you may not come into temptation; the spirit is willing, but the flesh is weak. (Mark 14:32–38)

In verses 33 to 34 above, the distress of Christ's flesh in facing what was to come was so intense He said He was "grieved to the point of death." In other words, the terror of the upcoming events was so heavy upon Him, He wished He could die rather than go through with the Father's will. We know from other references of the Gethsemane account that Jesus sweat drops of blood as a result of the turmoil within Him. This is a very real example of our flesh screaming within us to the extent that at times we feel as though we cannot go on.

We must be determined not to give into the flesh no matter how bad we feel or how hard it is. The flesh's strategy is to make us so miserable that we will ignore the direction of the Lord. Nevertheless, once our will has clearly made the decision to yield to the spirit in a particular battle, the struggle is over.

An example of the power of the release of the will is recorded in Mark 14:36. Jesus was in such a severe struggle between His flesh and spirit that He asked His disciples to support Him in this battle with prayer. When Christ was finally able to tell His Father, "not what I will, but what You will," the victory was won! As an act of His will, our Lord chose to do the will of the Father—despite what it would cost Him.

This is confirmed in verse 41 of the same chapter where Christ tells Peter, James, and John, "It is enough; the hour has come; behold, the Son of Man is being betrayed into the hands of sinners." What was enough? The time for the disciples to be praying was over because our Lord's will had yielded to the spirit. His flesh had lost the battle. He was ready to willingly be betrayed into the hands of His enemies.

Sometimes the flesh's insistence to get its own way will wear on us for days, weeks, or even months. However, as we consistently take a stand of faith in what the Bible teaches about the exchange of our old nature for Christ's nature, the strength of the flesh in the area we are battling will start to weaken. Winning one of these battles is equivalent to taking a city in the land of Canaan.

Just remember, in the battle against our flesh there is an endless number of strongholds. Even though the strength of the flesh does weaken and there are eventually fewer battles, the flesh will always be a foe until we are delivered out of these mortal bodies. In order to win the battle of the flesh against the spirit, you will have to be violent in your fight against sin. You will have to hate "even the garment polluted by the flesh" (Jude 1:23).

The need for us to not allow any trace of our self-life to rise up without aggressive opposition is emphasized in the possessing of the Promised Land. We see the strict instructions the Lord gave to Moses in Numbers 33.

> Then the LORD spoke to Moses in the plains of Moab by the Jordan opposite Jericho, saying, "Speak to the sons of Israel and say to them, When you cross over the Jordan into the land of Canaan, then you shall drive out all the inhabitants of the land from before you, and destroy all their figured stones, and destroy all their molten images and demolish all their high places; and you shall take possession of the land and live in it, for I have given the land to you to possess it. And you shall inherit the land by lot according to your families; to the larger you shall give more inheritance, and to the smaller you shall give less inheritance. Wherever the lot falls to anyone, that shall be his. You shall inherit according to the tribes of your fathers. But if you do not drive out the inhabitants of the land from before you, then it shall come about that those whom you let remain of them will become as pricks in your eyes and as thorns in your sides, and they shall trouble you in the land in which you live. And it shall come about that as I plan to do to them, so I will do to you." (Numbers 33:50–56)

The inhabitants of the land of Canaan are another type of the strongholds in our flesh that must be completely driven out. We often desire to remove the big areas of our lives that "self" is in control of, while remaining content to live with our less-debilitating, fleshly tendencies. We know that strongholds such as addictions, anger, and lust must go in order for us to live comfortably. Yet, when we become free of the more controlling and embarrassing habits of the flesh, it is easy to ignore the fine-tuning of the Holy Spirit. Regretfully, at this point in our spiritual growth, it is easy to allow the areas of the flesh we are content to live with to remain.

In Numbers 33:52, the Lord gave Moses a list of the things that were to be removed completely from the land. This list included the high places, which were pagan altars literally built at high geographical locations. We can safely presume the heathen inhabitants of the land thought the higher they could get, the more likely it would be that they would get the attention of their gods. In order to safeguard against idolatry, the Israelites were instructed to sacrifice to the One True God at only one place, which was Jerusalem. However, instead of unquestioning obedience to the Law of God, Israel saved certain pagan altars at the high places to use for sacrifices to Jehovah. They disobeyed God and left a door of temptation open by leaving some of the high-place altars intact.

We are likely to fall into disobedience against the known will of God if we compromise by allowing "little foxes" to remain in our lives (Song of Solomon 2:15). The little foxes are the ones that ruin the fruit of the vine. They may not eat all the fruit, but they spoil the quality. The little foxes of fleshly indulgence we allow will hinder the fruit of the Spirit in our lives.

We use compromise and rationalization to keep the high places of our lives intact. The Israelites compromised in their obedience to the clear command of God by not driving out every inhabitant of the land. Since heathen people were allowed to cohabitate with God's children, the high places remained available for sacrifices to heathen idols.

Most likely, the Israelites rationalized they would be more faithful in their required sacrifices to the Lord if they did not have to go to Jerusalem. Leaving the high places made serving Jehovah God easier—as well as more appeasing to their heathen neighbors. This decision made sense when it came to time management, but it wasn't obedience. God's word clearly teaches that "to obey is better than sacrifice" (1 Samuel 15:22).

Compromise and rationalization mean certain defeat in the battle against the flesh. We must destroy every lofty thing that challenges unwavering obedience to the revealed will of God. These high places or footholds of the flesh will rob us of the abundant life that Jesus died to give us. We may live quite peaceably for years with these and other inhabitants of the land, but if we choose to do so, we will fall short of kingdom life. Because the Israelites allowed some of the inhabitants of Canaan to remain, they never received all the Lord intended for them in the land of promise. We, too, will not experience the Kingdom of Heaven on earth without relentlessly driving out every attitude that is contrary to the clear teaching of scripture or is opposed to the quiet prompting of the Holy Spirit in our hearts.

The last verse in Numbers 33 makes an amazing statement. In reference to the driving out of the inhabitants of the land, the Lord says, "That as I plan to do to them, so I will do to you." In other words, if His people were not faithful in driving out all the inhabitants of the land, the Israelites would have to experience the judgment of the Lord along with the heathen. What does this mean for you and me?

Galatians 6:6–7 teaches the New Testament version of this truth.

> Do not be deceived, God is not mocked; for whatever a man sows, this he will also reap. For the one who sows to his own flesh shall from the flesh reap corruption, but the one who sows to the Spirit shall from the Spirit reap eternal life. (Galatians 6:6–7)

When we yield to the flesh instead of to the spirit, we are allowing an inhabitant of the land to remain. When Galatians 6 refers to sowing to the flesh, it is the same concept as yielding to the flesh, and what we plant is what we reap or harvest. When we plant fleshly seeds, we "reap corruption," which is a decline in the quality of life.

This brings us back to the truth God told the Israelites in Numbers 33—that what He planned to do to the inhabitants of the land, He would have to do to them (Numbers 33:56). Since His people were content to live with the heathen of the land—who represent the flesh—they would share in the same decline in the quality of life as the unbelievers they chose to live with. God was not able to give them all He intended to give them in the land, because the heathen could not share the children's bread. When we consciously allow our flesh to rule over the Spirit of God, Who dwells within us, we will reap the same quality of life as an unbeliever in the areas in which the flesh is allowed to reign. On the other hand, if we sow or plant according to the Spirit, we will "reap eternal life," which is equivalent to Christ's life, abundant life, or kingdom life.

Christ's life was placed within us at new birth, but new birth is not a guarantee of experiencing abundant life. Abundant life will only be ours in proportion to our faithfulness in driving out the inhabitants of the land.

The Battle from Without—Satan and Hordes from Hell

The battle from within is the battle of the flesh against the spirit. The battle from without is against the enemy of our souls, Satan, and his hordes of hell.

> Put on the full armor of God, that you may be able to stand firm against the schemes of the devil. For our struggle is not against flesh and blood, but against the rulers, against the powers, against the world forces of this darkness, against the spiritual forces of wickedness in the heavenly places. Therefore take up the full armor of God, that you may be able to resist in the evil day, and having done everything, to stand firm. (Ephesians 6:11–13)

The spiritual armor that is ours can be thought of as a literal suit of armor, which is Jesus. When we were "baptized into Christ Jesus" (Romans 6:3), we were placed "in Him" (Ephesians 1:7). Inside this armor, we have all the protection described in Ephesians 6. However, this armor is appropriated by faith—through which it becomes experiential. Faith rises up as we meditate on the word of God and gain a full understanding of our inheritance in Christ. Faith can then stand on the word, and we will triumph over the enemy's attacks from a position of being fitted with Christ as our armor. The position that gives us the "quietness and confidence" (Isaiah 30:15, KJV) to stand before any principality or power can never be based on our own self-righteousness or performance but must be fixed only on the truth that we are "in Christ."

Similar to the tactics of our flesh, Satan and his army are very subtle, clever, and persistent. We must be forceful and steadfast in our stand against the powers of darkness—offensively, as well as defensively.

One offensive strategy is to continually renew our minds through the word of God. The more we know the truth (John 14:6), the more we will recognize the schemes of the enemy.

> For though we walk in the flesh, we do not war according to the flesh, for the weapons of our warfare are not of the flesh, but divinely powerful for the destruction of fortresses. We are destroying speculations and every lofty thing raised up against the knowledge of God, and we are taking every thought captive to the obedience of Christ. (2 Corinthians 10:3–5)

We have already covered the importance of being led by the spirit rather than the flesh, but walking after the spirit is also an offensive strategy in spiritual warfare. When we walk after the spirit, we are abiding in Christ and we experience our Heavenly Father's protection. In this position, nothing can touch us apart from the lifting of the force field of His love. He may choose in His divine wisdom to allow the enemy to touch us, but we can be protected from onslaughts of the enemy we would not have to experience if we would only choose to walk in surrender and obedience.

The Sabbath Rest

The land of Canaan must be taken by force, but ironically, Canaan is also a picture of the "Sabbath rest."

There remains therefore a Sabbath rest for the people of God. For the one who has entered His rest has himself also rested from his works, as God did from His. (Hebrews 4:9–10)

The topic of rest seems out of place in a chapter on the violent taking the Kingdom of Heaven. Nevertheless, rest is synonymous with victory in the land. We cannot enter the land until we come to the end of all of our schemes, striving, manipulation, and other methods by which we attempt to control the circumstances of our lives. The one who has entered the "rest" God designed for His people has ceased from his own works.

Canaan is a type of total dependence on the Lord. Left to themselves, there was no way the Israelites would have been able to conquer the land. In their own strength, they would have been overwhelmed and defeated. The report of the ten spies—upon their initial return from spying out the land—was accurate.

There also we saw the Nephilim [the sons of Anak are part of the Nephilim]; and we became like grasshoppers in our own sight, and so we were in their sight. (Numbers 13:33)

In order to be victorious, they had to be totally dependent on God for the victory and had to acknowledge their own inability to bring to pass what God had promised. The ten spies had related an accurate account of what they saw in the land. There were giants in Canaan, and the Israelites were like grasshoppers compared to the Nephilim. From what they could see, there was not a chance they could overcome the giants that inhabited the land. They would only be able to enter the 'land of the promises of God' by believing in what God said He would do.

We will not enter the "rest" that characterizes Canaan or the Kingdom of God until we give up on self-effort. This includes self-effort exerted in order to please God. When we no longer even try to accomplish anything in our own strength, we have reached the position that must be attained, which is desperation. There is a place in the spirit where we are so worn-out, frustrated, and disillusioned with our own attempts at running our life that we want nothing to do with a "garment spotted by the flesh" (Jude 1:23). When we finally know deep inside our hearts that any self-effort will fail us, we are finally ready to enter God's rest by ceasing from our own works.

Rest and forcefulness seem to be contradictory, but to walk in the Kingdom of God, we must understand this paradox. Reviewing the nature of the flesh will help in our understanding of what seems to be an oxymoron. Our old man ruled our lives until the day we were born again. The flesh is the part of us that was trained by the old man and still wants life to go on as usual. The only way our old patterns of living are changed is by aggressively renewing our minds and choosing to yield to the spirit—no matter what our flesh says or desires. Our 'self-life' is a crafty foe and will try to deceive us to keep from losing control. Only belief in what the bible tells us about our new nature will give us the strength to stand against the flesh when 'common sense' says there is no hope of change or deliverance, or when the flesh has convinced us that its way is God's way.

The Battle

The battle in our unrenewed minds, unbridled will, and uncontrolled emotions must be fought violently in order to overcome. The more battles we win, the more peace or rest we will experience. We work out our own salvation with fear and trembling at the same time we fight to enter His rest. If you have never experienced the violent fight between your flesh and spirit, you may have never posed a significant challenge to 'self's' attempt to rule your life. Until you identify with Christ's death, burial, resurrection, and ascension, you will not have sufficiently intimidated the giant of 'self' to cause it to rise up. Similar to demonic forces, the flesh will play dead so that we will feel content—not recognizing our problem—and, consequently, continue on with good intentions while still operating in the energy of the flesh. The battle does not begin until the death sentence is issued.

Kingdom life cannot be experienced in our natural strength but is the outflow of the rule and reign of Christ within us. We will experience the Kingdom of God as we "die daily" (1 Corinthians 15:31) and allow Jesus to live His life through us. The Israelites did not experience the battles of taking the land until they crossed the Jordan. The wilderness was a place of apathy and ease. They had to fight to take Canaan, however, and we must war to enter His rest! Salvation is a free gift, but the Kingdom of God is taken by force!

CHAPTER 4

Children Live in the Kingdom

Our walk with God is alive and fulfilling. With Him, every day is new—fresh with insight and deeper intimacy. Everything we receive from the Lord is ever increasing—bigger (more encompassing), better, and more beautiful! All we have in Him was given to us at new birth but is experienced layer by layer as we appropriate His word and spend time in His presence. As we seek Him with all of our heart, He continuously brings forth more and more insight into His written word and an ever-deepening knowledge of His ways and His kingdom.

The many characteristics of childlikeness are also revealed to us in layers. As we look at the virtues of a child, we will gain an even greater understanding of the Kingdom of God. We are going to begin our study of the bible's teaching on childlikeness with the Lord's instruction in Mark 10.

> And they were bringing children to Him so that He might touch them; and the disciples rebuked them. But when Jesus saw this, He was indignant and said to them, "Permit the children to come to Me; do not hinder them; for the Kingdom of God belongs to such as these. Truly I say to you, whoever does not receive the Kingdom of God like a child shall not enter it at all." And He took them in His arms and began blessing them, laying His hands upon them. (Mark 10:13–16)

For years, I believed this passage meant Jesus gave preference to children. I thought He rebuked the disciples because they did not understand the special worth of a child. Finally, after studying similar passages, I realized Jesus was emphasizing the need for childlike faith to enter the kingdom.

My problem then became—what is childlike faith? Sometimes, the statements we make as Christians are correct but hard to apply to everyday life. Childlike faith certainly is a part of inheriting the Kingdom of God, but how do we get it? I had heard numerous pat answers—none of which felt quite right.

Defining "Kingdom"

Finally, I came across the definition of the Kingdom of God/ Kingdom of Heaven I now embrace. With my previous understanding of the Kingdom of God as the place where believers go when they die, it had been very difficult to understand Jesus' words in regards to children. The newly discovered definition, from the *Vine's Expository Dictionary of New Testament Words*, gave new clarity to much of what Jesus taught. The definition reads, "The sovereign rule of God, with a people over whom He reigns, and a realm in which the power of His reign is experienced."[4]

With this definition in mind, we must understand kingdom life is only experienced to the degree we allow God—in His sovereignty—to rule and reign in our lives. We only realize the Kingdom of God to the extent the Spirit of Christ rules our hearts.

Since the kingdom is "at hand," or here among us, the next hurdle was to grasp an understanding of how to walk in the kingdom on a continual basis. Mark 10:14 says, "The Kingdom of God belongs to such as these." If something belongs to us, we can experience it as we choose—even on a moment-by-moment basis. If the kingdom "belongs to such as these," studying the ways of children can teach us how to walk day-by-day in the kingdom.

[4.] Vine's Expository Dictionary of New Testament Words

The state of kingdom living is given several names in scripture. One name the Lord gives those who experience His kingdom is that of a "disciple." Another name is "overcomer." One more term is His "bride." These foundational truths are necessary in order to glean kingdom life principles from the attributes of a child.

Consider a Child

An understanding of childlikeness will give us insight into the teachings of Christ. However, keep in mind not every aspect of child-likeness is comparable to kingdom life.

We'll start our study of a child's nature by thinking of a very young child—before he or she has developed a will of his/her own. This analogy is not for the purpose of developing doctrine but is instead aimed at helping our finite minds grasp infinite truth. Regretfully, the older we get, the less we exhibit the attributes of kingdom life displayed in the very young. Since the flesh is the part of our soul—mind, will, and emotions—that was programmed by our old nature, the older a child gets, the more he or she has developed the characteristics of the "old man" that must be "put off" (Colossians 3:9, KJV).

Nurturing Dependence on God

The very thought of being childlike is a stumbling block to most adults. This is especially demeaning to those who consider themselves capable and responsible. Since one of the major attributes needed to experience kingdom life is total dependence on Jesus, it is hard for most adults to come to this place. Our Lord, Himself, said He could do nothing apart from the Father (John 5:19), and we can do nothing apart from Jesus. When we are born again, our old man is crucified with Christ, and we receive a new nature or a new life. Jesus is literally the 'life force' within us. Anything done apart from dependence on Him is of the flesh—no matter how good or benefi-cial the outward appearance.

This dependence on the life of Christ within is considered weakness by many well-meaning Christians who have not yet come to the end of their own resources. Our eyes are truly blinded to how self-sufficient we really are until our loving Heavenly Father orchestrates events in our lives to break us of our self-sufficiency. These carefully arranged circumstances are designed to bring us to a place of desperation. In that divinely appointed place, we have the choice to find a 'fire escape'—a fleshly way out—or to depend totally on our Lord.

On the contrary, a child does not have to be brought to the point of desperation. Children are totally dependent on their caretakers and are naturally aware they cannot take care of themselves. We are born dependent on others and feel secure in that position.

A very young child also has not developed a will of his or her own. In contrast, we as adults must go through the breaking process of becoming a grain of wheat that is willing to fall to the ground and die. This is the moment-by-moment process of surrendering our will to the will of God.

> Truly, truly, I say to you, unless a grain of wheat falls into the earth and dies, it remains alone; but if it dies, it bears much fruit. (John 12:24)

This breaking process will continue until we get to the point where Jesus was in the Garden of Gethsemane ("Father, if You are willing, remove this cup from Me; yet not My will, but Yours be done" [Luke 22:42]) or until we rebel against the processing of God and go our own way ("There is a way which seems right to a man, But its end is the way of death" [Proverbs 14:12 and Proverbs 16:25]).

Many of us truly think we are totally dependent on God until we find ourselves at a divinely planned 'Y' in the path of life. Our Father will purposely bring us to the place where, seemingly, the only way off the painful path He has chosen for us is for us to take back control of our lives. At this fork in the road, those who have not really come to the end of themselves will instinctively grab for control of their lives without even knowing it. Until our self-life is broken by the power of the cross, we will be open to self-deception. When confronted with a choice that is not 'our self's' desire, we will usually convince ourselves our choice is God's choice, rather than face the resulting consequences of God's leading.

Self-Centeredness and Surrender

To gain further understanding as to the way of a child, we need to think about how our own willfulness was developed. We started at birth with the need to be fed and kept warm and clean. We then began to develop something that would resemble a family tree. To our basic needs, we added the way we wanted to be fed, the times we felt like eating, and—of course—the things we did and did not want to eat. In addition to how we wanted to be fed, we added what we thought we needed in order to be comfortable and also added our demands for cleanliness. Our root system of desires became larger as we grew and experienced more available options in life.

The point of this analogy is that from our basic beginnings, we added more and more branches to our tree until we soon had a very complicated set of dreams, desires, and perceived needs. In order to experience kingdom life, all of our self-centered dreams, desires, and perceived needs—developed since childhood—must be relinquished for the purposes of the Lord. He may not choose to rearrange our root system or remove any of the branches of our 'tree of life,' but we must be willing to allow Him to do so.

There is a pivotal time for each of us when we must consciously surrender control of our lives to Him. Even after that initial surrender, however, we will be placed in situation after situation where we will have to choose either the Lord's way or our way. This is the way of the cross. When we decide to choose God's way, we "take up" our "cross" (Matthew 16:24). As the late Oswald Chambers stated, "The cross is the pain involved in doing the will of God."

The more our will is given over to the Father, the more we become like little children. The things that used to be of utmost importance do not seem to matter much anymore. As we consistently choose to yield our will to the will of the Father, we will gradually find ourselves with more peace and joy. We will also find ourselves much more content—not because the things we desired were ripped out of our hands but due to the grace of God giving us the power to open our hands and release the desires of our hearts to Him. As the grace of God simplifies our lives, we will find ourselves becoming more childlike, and as we become more childlike, we realize the Kingdom of God is truly "at hand."

Relationships
Part of the Family

Looking at the relationships in children's lives and their responses to life can help further illustrate the comparisons between a child and the characteristics needed to experience the Kingdom of God on earth.

First of all, a child is part of a family. We are members of the family of God. We didn't earn the right to become a part of God's family, but it was a privilege extended to us because of our Heavenly Father's desire to have a family of sons and daughters with the same nature as His Son, Jesus.

> Now to the one who works, his wage is not credited as a favor, but as what is due. But to the one who does not work, but believes in Him who justifies the ungodly, his faith is credited as righteousness. (Romans 4:4–5)

Most Christians acknowledge they did not earn the right to be a child of God, but as Christians, we still have a strong tendency to feel as though we must earn the right to be accepted into the family of God. We tend to feel guilty when we do not keep the list of dos and don'ts we think God expects of us, and we allow the enemy of our souls to torment us with guilt and condemnation. In contrast, earning the right to be a member of the family never even crosses a child's mind.

Not only do most Christians have deep-seated insecurities in regards to God's acceptance of them, but most 'adult' or 'mature'

Christians will usually even scorn one who walks in the peace of total acceptance, as a child does. The thought of the freedom of childlike acceptance seems irresponsible or irrational when it is actually vital to an intimate relationship with God.

Chosen and Accepted

The second relational truth about children is they feel wanted. Ideally, our parents had us because they desired children. We had nothing to do with being a part of our family. In the case of the family of God, our Father wanted us to be His children so much that He arranged for our adoption. We do have to choose to accept the Father's invitation to become His children, but the provision was all His doing.

> But when the fullness of the time came, God sent forth His Son, born of a woman, born under the Law, so that He might redeem those who were under the Law, that we might receive the adoption as sons. Because you are sons, God has sent forth the Spirit of His Son into our hearts, crying, "Abba! Father!" Therefore you are no longer a slave, but a son; and if a son, then an heir through God. (Galatians 4:4–7)

> For all who are being led by the Spirit of God, these are sons of God. For you have not received a spirit of slavery leading to fear again, but you have received a spirit of adoption as sons by which we cry out, "Abba! Father!" The Spirit Himself testifies with our spirit that we are children of God. (Romans 8:14–16)

> Blessed be the God and Father of our Lord Jesus Christ, who hath blessed us with all spiritual blessings in heavenly places in Christ: According as he hath chosen us in him before the foundation of the world, that we should be holy and without blame before him in love: Having predestinated us unto the adoption of children by Jesus Christ to himself, according to the good pleasure of his will, To the praise of the glory of his grace,

wherein He hath made us accepted in the beloved. (Ephesians 1:3–6, KJV)

Ephesians chapter 1 speaks of our being predestined to be adopted as children of God. However, with the whole counsel of God in mind, we know that although we were predestined to be His children, we also had to choose to accept His offer. To our mortal minds, these two truths seem to conflict, but both are equally true. From the desire of His heart, our Heavenly Father initiated our adoption in heaven, but it became a reality on earth when we ran into His open arms.

The Image of Our Father

Children also resemble their mother and father in appearance and behavior. Heredity automatically bestows a likeness between children and their parents. They look like their parents due to common genes, act like their parents through inherited personality and a shared environment, and have in common many of the same gifts and talents. If you have seen the children—to some extent—you have seen the parents.

Even in the case of adoption, it is a proven fact that the environment in which we are reared affects many of our behavioral characteristics. Still today, debate continues as to whether heredity or environment effects our development most. As we walk in the environment or 'atmosphere of God,' we are gradually changed into the image of Christ, which is the image of our Father.

Even though we are adopted by God and are not children by natural birth, when we are born again, His likeness is implanted in us through the impartation of our new nature. The heredity portion of being a child of God is birthed within us—giving us the characteristics of natural children.

For in Him we live and move and exist, as even some of your own poets have said, "For we also are His children." Being then the children of God, we ought not to think that the Divine

Nature is like gold or silver or stone, an image formed by the art
and thought of man. (Acts 17:28–29)

Even before we were born again and became children of God,
we were created in His image. The "image of God" gave us all of the
basic attributes Adam was created with.

God created man in His own image, in the image of God He
created him; male and female He created them. (Genesis 1:27)

The divine nature we received at new birth restored the spiritual
part Adam lost because of his sin. Mankind was made in the image
of God so our Heavenly Father would have many children in the
likeness of His Son, Jesus.

But now Christ has been raised from the dead, the first fruits
of those who are asleep. For since by a man came death, by a
man also came the resurrection of the dead. For as in Adam all
die, so also in Christ all will be made alive. But each in his own
order: Christ the first fruits, after that those who are Christ's at
His coming. (1 Corinthians 15:20–23)

Jesus is the firstfruits of many brethren (similar to one spirit
but multiple fruit of the Spirit). The meaning of firstfruits does not
speak of Christ as first with a second and third to come, but firstfruits
means there will be many more exactly like the first.

By this, love is perfected with us, so that we may have confidence in the day of judgment; because as He is, so also are we in
this world. (1 John 4:17)

Our Heavenly Father made such an all-inclusive provision in
our adoption as sons that He loves us even as His only begotten
Son. When we accepted Christ as our Savior, the life of His Son was
supernaturally birthed into our temporary bodies—which are only

"earthsuits."[5] This was accomplished in order to give the Father many more children like His Son.

Sons, Not Slaves

Another relational similarity between Christians and children is that we are sons of God, not slaves.

In the parable of the prodigal son, the elder brother was furious that his father had received his younger brother back with open arms, had restored his rights in the family, and had thrown him a big party. The older brother did not have the heart of a child and had served his father out of compulsion, rather than love. His heart is revealed in Luke 15.

> But he answered and said to his father, "Look! For so many years I have been serving you and I have never neglected a command of yours; and yet you have never given me a young goat, so that I might celebrate with my friends; but when this son of yours came, who has devoured your wealth with prostitutes, you killed the fattened calf for him." And he said to him, "Son, you have always been with me, and all that is mine is yours." (Luke 15:29–31)

Children typically do not earn their inheritance from their parents, but it becomes theirs solely because they are part of the family. The elder brother not only served the father with the heart of a hired hand, but he also did not live in the joy and confidence of all that was his just because he was his father's son.

Since we are sons and not slaves, we have been given so much that we cannot even begin to comprehend our inheritance from our Heavenly Father. Our inheritance from our Father is the Kingdom of God and all it includes. Scripture describes our position as sons and daughters of God as "fellow heirs" with Christ. This is not the position of a slave!

---

5. *Lifetime Guarantee*, Bill Gillham

And if children, heirs also, heirs of God and fellow heirs with Christ, if indeed we suffer with Him so that we may also be glorified with Him. (Romans 8:17)

Safe and Secure

The last relational similarity between a child and one of God's children is that they are provided for and protected. Emotionally healthy children always look to their parents to 'make everything better.'

And He said to His disciples, "For this reason I say to you, do not worry about your life, as to what you will eat; nor for your body, as to what you will put on. For life is more than food, and the body more than clothing. Consider the ravens, for they neither sow nor reap; they have no storeroom nor barn, and yet God feeds them; how much more valuable you are than the birds! And which of you by worrying can add a single hour to his life's span? If then you cannot do even a very little thing, why do you worry about other matters? Consider the lilies, how they grow: they neither toil nor spin; but I tell you, not even Solomon in all his glory clothed himself like one of these. But if God so clothes the grass in the field, which is alive today and tomorrow is thrown into the furnace, how much more will He clothe you? You men of little faith! And do not seek what you will eat and what you will drink, and do not keep worrying. For all these things the nations of the world eagerly seek; but your Father knows that you need these things. But seek His kingdom, and these things will be added to you. Do not be afraid, little flock, for your Father has chosen gladly to give you the kingdom." (Luke 12:22–32)

As adults, we have a tendency to worry about life. Whereas, scripture is very clear that if we can't add even another hour to our lifespan, what good does it do us to worry about life? We like to think—that as mature adults—we have to constantly have life's issues on our mind, when the exact opposite is true! In order to regularly experience the Kingdom of God, we are to take no thought for tomorrow, nor even for the next moment—unless we are in the process of making specific plans.

> So do not worry about tomorrow; for tomorrow will care for itself. Each day has enough trouble of its own. (Matthew 6:34)

This is not being irresponsible. We must renew our minds to the word of God, rather than to what makes sense to us. His ways are "higher" than ours. We need to surrender our ways of thinking and even our way of 'doing life.'

> "For My thoughts are not your thoughts, Nor are your ways My ways," declares the LORD. "For as the heavens are higher than the earth, So are My ways higher than your ways And My thoughts than your thoughts." (Isaiah 55:8–9)

We will never walk daily in the Kingdom of Heaven without total abandonment to God. We desperately need to seek the "counsel of His will" (Ephesians 1:11) rather than the way we think is right.

> Many plans are in a man's heart, But the counsel of the LORD will stand. (Ephesians 1:11)

The rationalization of why our way is necessary can be an excuse for not yielding to the Lord's instruction and direction for our lives. Much of what we—as responsible adults—consider necessary is really no more than worry.

A child expects to be protected and knows he is going to be provided for. In order to experience the Kingdom of Heaven, we must walk this earth as a child. This is a real deathblow to our pride. Childlikeness is ridiculous to many. Very few Christians will walk in the simplicity of childlike faith that will allow them to overcome the world.

But I am afraid that, as the serpent deceived Eve by his craftiness, your minds will be led astray from the simplicity and purity of devotion to Christ. (2 Corinthians 11:3)

A Child's Response

We have looked at the similarities in the relationship between a child and his parents—as compared with our relationship to our Heavenly Father. Now, we can gain great insight into God's ways by studying how a child responds to life.

One characteristic of a child that can aid us in spiritual maturity is to be honest about our feelings. This is not blurting out all we feel and all we know, but it is an end to self-preservation and an increase in honesty with God.

We need to be honest with ourselves—and with God—as to our conditioned responses in three major areas of life. First of all, a child does not play emotional or 'mind games' with others. Secondly, children do not hide behind walls of self-protection. Finally, they do not live life in continual fear (as we have said before, these analogies are for our insight and not to try to prove that our examples are always true in the life of every child). Again, children show us God's way, as opposed to how we have a tendency to 'do life.'

Unpretentious Honesty

The *Emperor's New Clothes* by Hans Christian Anderson portrays the perfect example of a child's honesty compared to the developed self-protection of the more mature.

There once was an emperor who was so vain that in order to show off his lavish wardrobe, he changed his clothes every hour. A couple of crooks got the ingenious idea that they would present themselves to the king as fine tailors. Their plan was to convince the king that the suit they would make for him would be so soft and so fine that the fabric would appear invisible to anyone who was not 'too stupid and incompetent to appreciate its quality.'

Throughout the story, the characters involved—including the king—cannot see the suit but do not want to appear 'stupid and incompetent' by admitting they don't see the fabric. The crooks eventually convince the king to appear before his people in his new suit—even though even he thinks he looks naked in the suit.

As the king parades before his people, cries as to how wonderful his new suit is escalate from the crowd. Suddenly, a child cries out that the king is naked. The child is even rebuked by his father for appearing 'stupid and incompetent.' At long last, the honesty of the child catches on, and the outcry changes to the reality of the king's nakedness, which soon resounds throughout the crowd of people. (Author's Summarization)

The sadness of this story is that we, as Christians, often forsake truth for what we perceive others want to think or hear. In order to walk in the kingdom, we have to become absolutely honest with God—Who knows everything anyway—and with ourselves, which is often hard.

Part of our inability to be honest with ourselves is that we really do not know what is deep within our hearts. Years of hurt and pro-grammed responses have made us hypocritical to our own hearts.

> The heart is deceitful above all things, and desperately wicked: who can know it? (Jeremiah 17:9)

This deceitful (or polluted) heart is not our born again spirit but is the heart of flesh that was programmed by our old nature. The division of the soul from the spirit, through the application of the cross to our self-life, is our only hope for freedom from our 'self.'

> For the word of God is living and active and sharper than any two-edged sword, and piercing as far as the division of soul

and spirit, of both joints and marrow, and able to judge the thoughts and intentions of the heart. And there is no creature hidden from His sight, but all things are open and laid bare to the eyes of Him with whom we have to do. (Hebrews 4:12–13)

The "word" that is living and active in Hebrews 4:12 should actually be capitalized, as it is a reference to Christ—the Living Word. In the beginning of verse 13 above, within the phrase, "there is no creature hidden from His sight," the "His" is correctly capitalized. The life of the Lord Jesus Himself is resident in every believer. As we identify with Christ—Who is our true identity—His life will divide between our soul and spirit. As our soul is separated from our spirit, we will begin to see what is really in our hearts. At this point in our spiritual growth, we will then be faced with the choice to ask God to give us the grace to be set free from what is revealed or to begin to 'play games,' build walls, and/or live in the fear of reality.

Hidden Agendas, Hardened Hearts

In addition to honesty, children also do not have hidden agendas. As adults, we have spent most of our lives 'maturing' our self-life. Our 'self' is constantly engaged in providing for its own needs and desires—including self-protection. 'Self' is the control center of our flesh, and it has a detailed agenda as to how it wants its needs met. When we have an agenda, we cannot even trust ourselves.

Until the soul is separated from the spirit, it is very difficult to know the difference between 'self-motivation' and the prompting of the Spirit of God. It is also hard to differentiate between the voice of the flesh, the many voices of demonic entities, and the voice of the Holy Spirit. We greatly need to desire the separation of our soul and spirit—above all else and despite the cost. This separation can free us from self-preservation and begin our restoration back to having the heart of a child, which has no agenda.

The next problem adults develop is hardness-of-heart. Years of self-refinement and protecting our agendas cause us to ignore the promptings of the Holy Spirit. Each and every time we ignore the

Spirit's tug on our heart, a part of our heart is hardened. If we continue to ignore the voice and nudging of the Lord, we are in danger of eventually allowing our heart to be completely hardened—even to the place where we no longer see the need for Christ as our Savior.

> For the wrath of God is revealed from heaven against all ungodliness and unrighteousness of men who suppress the truth in unrighteousness, because that which is known about God is evident within them; for God made it evident to them. For since the creation of the world His invisible attributes, His eternal power and divine nature, have been clearly seen, being understood through what has been made, so that they are without excuse. For even though they knew God, they did not honor Him as God or give thanks, but they became futile in their speculations, and their foolish heart was darkened. Professing to be wise, they became fools. (Romans 1:18–22)

> And just as they did not see fit to acknowledge God any longer, God gave them over to a depraved mind, to do those things which are not proper, being filled with all unrighteousness, wickedness, greed, evil; full of envy, murder, strife, deceit, malice; they are gossips, slanderers, haters of God, insolent, arrogant, boastful, inventors of evil, disobedient to parents, without understanding, untrustworthy, unloving, unmerciful; and although they know the ordinance of God, that those who practice such things are worthy of death, they not only do the same, but also give hearty approval to those who practice them. (Romans 1:28–32)

The opposite of the hardened heart is the pure heart of a child. A child's heart possesses a naiveté that is an affront to an adult. Since the words we speak come forth from our heart, the innocence and truth of the words of a child are at times 'feared' by adults (similar to *The Emperor's New Clothes*).

Those seeking a closer, more intimate walk with the Lord must desire this naiveté. In order to walk in such close communion with

Christ that we become an expression of Him on this earth, we will have to ask the Lord to reverse the hardness of our hearts.

As we "lie down in green pastures," and as the Lord "leads" us "beside quiet waters," the presence of the Lord "restores" our souls. With restored souls, we can then be guided "in the paths of righteousness for His name's sake" (Psalm 23:2–3). The restoring of our soul (our mind, will, and emotions) is part of the reversal of our hardened hearts.

Children are also very resilient. They have a tendency to forgive and forget quite easily. In order to walk this earth in the freedom and power of the presence of the Lord, we must develop a habit of immediate forgiveness and forgetting offenses against us. A crucial issue in walking without offense begins with where we set the focus of our minds.

> Therefore if you have been raised up with Christ, keep seeking the things above, where Christ is, seated at the right hand of God. Set your mind on the things above, not on the things that are on earth. (Colossians 3:1–2)

We must develop the practice of setting our mind on the things of the Lord whenever our mind does not have to be actively involved with the temporal.

> For who has known the mind and purposes of the Lord, so as to instruct Him? But we have the mind of Christ [to be guided by His thoughts and purposes]. (1 Corinthians 2:16, AMPC)

As we yield to the Holy Spirit, the river of life flows through our mind and the renewal of our mind begins. As we train ourselves to set our "mind on things above," the purposes for our own lives, as well as the purposes of God for this world, take the forefront in our thoughts.

Another result of our increasing mind-set "on things above" will be our ability to lose track of offenses against us. If, as an act of our will, we refuse to even entertain memories that breed unforgiveness in our hearts, the memories will quickly fade away. In fact, if we never tell anyone (including our spouse or best friend) the details of an offense, the facts will soon be forgotten and will never be allowed to turn into bitterness. This is freedom!

> A man's [moral] self shall be filled with the fruit of his mouth; and with the consequence of his words he must be satisfied [whether good or evil]. Death and life are in the power of the tongue, and they who indulge in it shall eat the fruit of it [for death or life]. (Proverbs 18:20–21, AMPC)

The words that come forth from our mouth fill our innermost being. Our words can either bring healing to our hearts or great brokenness to our soul and spirit. Sadly enough, if we should choose to continue down a path of self-inflicted wounds—without repentance—we could be crippled for life from our own thoughts and words.

If we are faithful to follow these disciplines, we will find ourselves walking in a continual grace of forgiveness. This allows us to experience the kingdom, as we walk this world, with the naiveté of a child who has never felt pain.

Children Enjoy Life

The previous characteristics of a child, as studied in this chapter, lead us to the next childlike attribute—children enjoy life. They appreciate the little things in life, usually go with the flow, and expect life to be fun. In contrast to a child, the painful experiences and the responsibilities of existence on this earth leave most adults dull and disillusioned.

Our personalities and life experiences give us varying degrees of optimism and pessimism. Ultimately, though, the renewal of our mind, will, and emotions is necessary to have childlike optimism. A popular framed poster reads, "The happiness of your life is in direct proportion to the character of your thoughts." Our emotions are reactors and feed off the stimulus of our thoughts and the events around us. The biblical version of this is, "For as he thinks in his heart, so is he" (Proverbs 23:7a). Another witness to this truth is, "As in water face reflects face, so the heart of man reflects man" (Proverbs 27:19).

We need to fill our lives with the truth of God's word so our minds will have positive thoughts for our emotions to react to. We need to be conformed into the image of Christ in order to begin to experience His heart, which will transform us from the inside out. Then, as our "heart" is, so will we be—full of peace and joy.

A major key to enjoying life is the surrender of our will to God's will. If we refuse to do this by demanding our rights and insisting on the way we want life to go, we can easily become miserable.

Two common misconceptions that keep us from enjoying life are unachieved goals and disappointed expectations. Goals are accomplishments we have the ability to bring to pass, and expectations are desires we would like to see happen but are beyond our control. If we look at expectations (over which we have no control) as goals, we will not be able to walk in childlike joy. Ultimately, the only 'safe' goals in life are the ones our Father has spoken to our hearts and confirmed as His will and destiny for us—for without Him we cannot achieve any goal.

When we surrender all our dreams, desires, and goals to the Lord, we release the demands we've placed on God. The resulting freedom in these areas will allow us to live in the kingdom, with the joy of a child and the authority of a son.

Children Bear the Image of Their Father

The 'adult' world we live in deeply desires a kingdom such as we are studying. However, such a kingdom will not be visible if we fail to allow ourselves to be childlike. They may never be drawn to the real thing—because it is rarely seen. Just think about the songs, phrases, commercials, and movies that attract the multitudes. Each and every day, people around us long to be a child again. They long to "don't worry—be happy" but would consider such an attitude irresponsible or immature.

Becoming childlike is a stumbling block to nearly every adult. It is crucial to not miss this important key to the Kingdom of Heaven through misconceptions of the kingdom. "Truly I say to you, unless you are converted and become like children, you will not enter the Kingdom of Heaven" (Matthew 18:3). You will not only fail to enter the Kingdom of Heaven unless you become as a child, but you will also not be able to continue to walk in and experience the kingdom unless you remain childlike.

Do not lightly dismiss this truth! Your own pride could rob you of the wonderful plans God has for your life.

> Humble yourselves therefore beneath the mighty hand of God, so that at the right time He may set you on high. (1 Peter 5:6, 1912 Weymouth NT)

The Lord is currently calling His people higher—to rule and reign with Him in heavenly places. However, in order to go higher, we must go lower—choosing to humble ourselves by becoming as little children in the sight of all heaven and earth. My prayer for you is that the Lord's requirement of childlikeness will not be such a stumbling block to you that you "fall short of the glory of God" (Romans 3:23).

CHAPTER 5

The Kingdom of Light

> This is the judgment, that the Light has come into the world, and men loved the darkness rather than the Light, for their deeds were evil. For everyone who does evil hates the Light, and does not come to the Light for fear that his deeds will be exposed. But he who practices the truth comes to the Light, so that his deeds may be manifested as having been wrought in God.
>
> —John 3:19–21

The Kingdom of God is light, and there is no darkness in the kingdom. Consequently, the Kingdom of God is only expressed in our lives in the areas that darkness no longer remains in our souls.

There is a light available Who can show us everything in our lives that is not of His kingdom, and yet darkness remains—this is great judgment! All we need for life and godliness was placed within us at new birth, and yet we choose to fall short of the glory of God.

> It is time for judgment to begin with the household of God. (1 Peter 4:17a)

Why is this judgment to us? Are we possibly unaware these dark areas exist? Jesus' reply would be, "Light has come into the world, and men loved the darkness rather than the Light, for their deeds were evil." Unequivocally—with all openness and without guile—light makes all things very clear. Yet, we choose darkness so that our evil deeds will not be exposed.

Evil is not exclusive to ax murderers and the like of Hitler. Evil is the nature of the Kingdom of Darkness, and good—as God would call it—exists only in the Kingdom of Light. That which is of the flesh is from the training of the "old man," which is the manifestation of the sinful nature we received from Adam. All we received from Adam belongs to the Kingdom of Darkness.

Good can come only from the Spirit of God within us, Who is the representative of the Kingdom of Light on this earth—"which is Christ in you, the hope of glory" (Colossians 1:27). That which is light comes from the "new man" (Ephesians 2:15), which is the new nature we received at new birth. Jesus Christ is the firstfruit of a new race—begotten of God for the intent of bringing His kingdom to earth, which includes His light.

Why would we choose to hide in darkness when the Light is in us? Our self-life manifests itself in clever, subtle ways in order to hide the motives behind our thoughts, words, and deeds. The instinct of self-preservation within us is so strong only the Word of God Himself can divide between our soul and spirit. Moreover, only the Spirit of God can give us the grace to side with illumined truth over our own selfish desires.

The Power of the Cross

Our co-crucifixion with Jesus Christ gave us power over sin, as well as the power over 'self.' The only hope for us to come to the end of ourselves, or to become 'selfless,' is to appropriate our death with Jesus Christ as the answer for every "sin which so easily entangles us" (Hebrews 12:1). As we "consider" ourselves "to be dead to sin, but alive to God in Christ Jesus" (Romans 6:11), our faith applies the work of the cross as a deathblow to 'self.'

By continually presenting ourselves as living sacrifices to God, we will gradually be freed from conforming to this world. Moreover, as we make the choice to not be conformed to this world, we will be transformed into the image of Christ—"from glory to glory" (2 Corinthians 3:18).

Once our will has chosen the position of "not my will Lord, but Your will—no matter what the cost," our self-life will remain under a death sentence until we become 'self-less.' Our self-life is the stronghold in us that makes us love darkness rather than light, for light exposes our selfishness. When our self-centeredness has been brought to an end through the application of the cross, we will no longer fear being exposed by the light.

Several years ago, the Lord let me see myself as an eagle flying into the sun, which was representative of 'the Son.' He told me to fly into the sun, since I really would not want anything the fire would consume. As I made the choice to fly into the sun, my eagle feathers turned to ashes and left only a featherless, gleaming gold eagle. Similar to Adam before the fall, I was a bare eagle but did not feel exposed. I was clothed with the glory of God, even as Adam and Eve before their knowledge of good and evil.

When we throw ourselves unreservedly into the 'Son'—in total dependence upon the mercy of God—we will love the light. There is freedom, joy, and peace in the light—along with all the Kingdom of God entails.

Which Kingdom Are You In?

In Colossians, we are told that Jesus "rescued us from the domain of darkness, and transferred us to the kingdom of His beloved Son" (Colossians 1:13). We must have a basic understanding that there are only two kingdoms—the Kingdom of Darkness and the Kingdom of Light. Satan is the ruler of the Kingdom of Darkness, and King Jesus rules the Kingdom of Light.

Before we were born again, we were citizens of the Kingdom of Darkness—no matter how 'good' we were. When you received Christ as your Savior, He "called you out of darkness into His marvelous light" (1 Peter 2:9b). This transfer of kingdoms was accomplished by

Jesus' exchange of His righteous nature for our sinful nature. When we received His life, we were flooded with light.

> Then Jesus again spoke to them, saying, "I am the Light of the world; he who follows Me will not walk in the darkness, but will have the Light of life." (John 8:12)

A person who is not redeemed by the blood of the Lamb cannot have light in Him. Conversely, if we are in Christ, we are in the light, even if we do not feel like it.

> This is the message we have heard from Him and announce to you, that God is Light, and in Him there is no darkness at all. If we say that we have fellowship with Him and yet walk in the darkness, we lie and do not practice the truth; but if we walk in the Light as He Himself is in the Light, we have fellowship with one another, and the blood of Jesus His Son cleanses us from all sin. (1 John 1:5–7)

This passage in 1 John has confused believers for years. If we do not have a basic understanding of one kingdom being light and the other being darkness, we will look at this section of scripture with a view of performance-based acceptance. Performance-based acceptance simply means that if I am able to live according to a certain set of rules (my performance) or am able to fulfill the expectations of my specific Christian group, I then consider myself acceptable to God. In other words, if I achieve my expectations, I believe I am walking in the light. If I fail to meet my criteria for 'successful Christian living,' I believe I am walking in darkness. This progression can lead to the ultimate conclusion: If I consider my performance to be in the 'darkness category,' I may not even feel born again!

This is not what John was saying. He was expressing the contrast between the Kingdom of Darkness and the Kingdom of Light. To understand this spiritual concept, let us imagine a physical example of darkness and light. If you have ever gone on a cave tour, they turn off all of the lights in the middle of the tour, leaving total darkness. Due to the many sources of light above ground, total darkness is hard to experience. However, in a cave, you literally cannot see your hand in front of your face. This total absence of light is darkness. If there is any light whatsoever, it is not a state of darkness.

So it is in the spiritual realm. If there is any light present in a person's heart, there is not a state of darkness but instead a state of diminished light. Since God is Light, there can only be light when His Spirit is present. If God is not present, then indeed there is total darkness. Many claim John teaches salvation by works, when the exact opposite is true. 1 John 1:5–7 is saying a person's performance is not what determines whether or not they are born again, but salvation is determined by whether they are in the light. The only way to walk in the light is to have the Light living within you, and self-effort can never produce real Light.

The Shadow of Death

Another passage of scripture describing the Kingdom of God as light, in contrast to the Kingdom of Satan as darkness, is in Matthew chapter 4.

> Now when Jesus heard that John had been taken into custody, He withdrew into Galilee; and leaving Nazareth, He came and settled in Capernaum, which is by the sea, in the region of Zebulun and Naphtali. This was to fulfill what was spoken through Isaiah the prophet: "THE LAND OF ZEBULUN AND THE LAND OF NAPHTALI, BY THE WAY OF THE SEA, BEYOND THE JORDAN, GALILEE OF THE GENTILES—THE PEOPLE WHO WERE SITTING IN DARKNESS SAW A GREAT LIGHT, AND THOSE WHO WERE SITTING IN THE LAND AND SHADOW OF DEATH, UPON THEM A LIGHT DAWNED." From that time Jesus began to preach and say, "Repent, for the Kingdom of Heaven is at hand." (Matthew 4:12–17)

In this account from the book of Matthew, Zebulun and Naphtali were in darkness. When Jesus came to their region, light dawned upon them. The presence of light, where there had formerly only been darkness, prompted Jesus to proclaim, "Repent, for the Kingdom of Heaven is at hand." The presence of light was a manifestation that the kingdom had come.

In Mark chapter 4, the people are shown as "sitting in the land and shadow of death." Satan's kingdom is permeated by death, and God's kingdom is ablaze with life. Zebulun and Naphtali were in darkness, which resulted in a condition of death. If we think of Death as an entity (Revelation 6:8), an entity casts a shadow. Moreover, there must be light for a shadow to be cast. Therefore, we can visualize Death at the entrance of the Kingdom of Darkness and the light shining from the Kingdom of Heaven causing Death to cast a shadow.

The inhabitants of Zebulun and Naphtali were living in the Kingdom of Darkness, under the shadow of Death. However, when Jesus entered the land, the light dawned upon them. This is a picture of new birth. Before we were born again, we were living in darkness in the land and in the shadow of death. Even though we may not have been aware of it, our inner man was as dark as an unlit cave. If God is not present, there is no light.

Then the day came when Jesus entered our land, and we were filled with light—even as the dawn fills the skies with radiance.

> But the path of the righteous is like the light of dawn, that
> shines brighter and brighter until the full day. (Proverbs 4:18)

We formerly lived under Satan's rule—in his kingdom—but with our transfer to the Kingdom of Heaven, the light flooded our souls.

> So we have the prophetic word made more sure, to which you
> do well to pay attention as to a lamp shining in a dark place,
> until the day dawns and the morning star arises in your hearts.
> (2 Peter 1:19)

The Morning Star Arises

When the morning star—Who is Jesus—arises in our hearts, it is as the breaking of the dawn. As the sun peaks above the horizon, rays of light are cast upon the land. When Christ's life is birthed within us, He—like the sun—shines glorious light across our souls. As we lay down our self-life and yield to His life, more light is allowed to bathe our mind, will, and emotions. The light from the morning star, reflecting from our spirit onto our soul, changes us into His image—from glory to glory.

> But we all, with unveiled face, beholding as in a mirror the glory of the Lord, are being transformed into the same image from glory to glory, just as from the Lord, the Spirit. (2 Corinthians 3:18)

As we continue to "walk in the Light as He Himself is in the Light" (1 John 1:7), the transformation of our mind, will, and emotions (soul) continues. Our soul will eventually be totally renewed and conformed to His image through this process.

We Were Darkness—Now We Are Light

There are numerous scriptures throughout the bible that portray the Kingdom of God as a Kingdom of Light. An understanding of these verses—without a revelation as to how these truths can help our spiritual growth—is not enough in itself. In one of Paul's exhortations to the Ephesians on what the Kingdom of Christ and God was like, he said these words:

> For this you know with certainty, that no immoral or impure person or covetous man, who is an idolater, has an inheritance in the kingdom of Christ and God. Let no one deceive you with empty words, for because of these things the wrath of God comes upon the sons of disobedience. Therefore do not be partakers with them; for you were formerly darkness, but now you

are Light in the Lord; walk as children of Light (for the fruit of the Light consists in all goodness and righteousness and truth), trying to learn what is pleasing to the Lord. Do not participate in the unfruitful deeds of darkness, but instead even expose them; for it is disgraceful even to speak of the things which are done by them in secret. But all things become visible when they are exposed by the light, for everything that becomes visible is light. For this reason it says, "Awake, sleeper, And arise from the dead, And Christ will shine on you." (Ephesians 5:5–14)

In order to understand these verses, a review of the definition of the Kingdom of Heaven is needed. According to *Vine's Expository Dictionary*, the Kingdom of Heaven is: "The sovereign rule of God, manifested in Christ to defeat His enemies, with a people over whom He reigns, and a realm in which the power of His reign is experienced." Our flesh and Satan are enemies of Christ and will only be defeated as Jesus is allowed to reign in our hearts.

Thinking of this definition, let's return to Ephesians chapter 5 where we are told, "No immoral or impure person or covetous man, who is an idolater, has an inheritance in the kingdom of Christ and God." With a parameter of performance-based acceptance, we have traditionally interpreted this verse as a list of things that could keep us out of heaven. The problem with this interpretation is that we are all capable of entertaining immoral or impure thoughts. Who has never coveted another's possessions, appearance, or lot in life? Who has never allowed anyone or anything to take the place of Jesus as the center of their life, thus making it an idol?

Even without a clear understanding of our imputed righteousness in Christ, this interpretation would not be plausible as God certainly did not send His Son to die for our sin only to then cast us away for fleshly thoughts or desires. Our own inability to attain righteousness is why we needed a Savior!

There are two ways to interpret this verse in consideration of the previous definition of the Kingdom of God and when taking into account our righteousness being a gift from God (2 Corinthians 5:21). The first interpretation in the context of Ephesians chapter 5 is that the list of spiritual conditions in verse 5 states that no "person" or "man" will enter the kingdom. This verse is not speaking of actions or performance but is a description of a person's nature. When a child of God, who is the righteousness of God in Christ Jesus (2 Corinthians 5:21), entertains an impure thought, he does not become an impure person. His nature is righteous because of Jesus. Therefore, he does not become impure in nature but is a person with the righteousness of Christ Jesus who has chosen to sin by entertaining an impure thought. Sin does not make a Christian a sinner.

The apostle Paul then goes on to tell the Ephesians, who are believers, to not be partakers with the sons of disobedience. In other words, it is possible for Christians to be partakers of these things, but they have a choice not to. Before we were born again, we were controlled by our sinful nature—no matter how good we looked. Romans 6:7 tells us that "he who has died is free from sin." We no longer have to sin. Sin is now a choice. That is why Paul tells the Ephesians to not partake in sinful things.

In Romans 5:8, he continues to teach the Ephesians they "were formerly darkness" but are now children of light. Consequently, they were to walk as children of light. Again, this teaches the reality of the Kingdom of Heaven being a Kingdom of Light. Before we were born again, we were "darkness"—our very being was darkness. Now, our innermost being is light—even if we choose to walk like children of darkness. How we walk does not change what we are.

The analogy of the Kingdom of Heaven to light continues in verse 13 with "all things become visible when they are exposed by the light." Shameful deeds or deeds that dishonor God are called deeds of darkness. When the presence of God turns the light on in our life, the nature of our deeds is revealed. Any awareness of sinfulness we have ever had is on account of the light that shines in the darkness. Since we know no one comes to Jesus unless they are drawn by the Father (John 6:44), we cannot even acknowledge our need for a savior until the Holy Spirit turns on the light, enabling us to see our sinful condition. This is consistent with 2 Corinthians 4:4, where we are told, "The God of this world has blinded the minds of the unbelieving, that they might not see the light of the gospel of the glory of Christ, who is the image of God."

Paul finishes this teaching on the Kingdom of God being light in Ephesians 5:14. The citizens of the Kingdom of Darkness are described as being asleep or dead. We know we were dead in our trespasses and sins before we came to Christ (Ephesians 2:1), and according to our earlier illustration of the "valley of the shadow of death," we were living in the Kingdom of Darkness, which is ruled by Death. We had a human spirit, but our spirit was dead to, or separated from, God. When the Light of the World shone on us and we chose to believe, we were made alive together with Him (Ephesians 2:5). When we were born again, the Holy Spirit made our human spirit alive (1 Peter 3:18) and the Light took residence within us. Where light is, darkness flees.

We Are the Light of the World

Scripture clearly teaches that the Kingdom of God is synonymous with light and Jesus is the source of light in the kingdom. Since the Light dwells within us, the next question to be considered is, what is our part as bearers of light in the kingdom? Matthew 5:14–16 describes our assignment. Jesus, Himself, left us these instructions:

> You are the light of the world. A city set on a hill cannot be hidden; nor does anyone light a lamp and put it under a basket, but on the lampstand, and it gives light to all who are in the house. Let your light shine before men in such a way that they may see your good works, and glorify your Father who is in heaven. (Matthew 5:14–16)

We know that Jesus is the Light of the World, but here in Matthew, the Lord is saying, "You are the light of the world." What an awesome responsibility! When Jesus left this earth in bodily form, He sent the Comforter—Who is the Holy Spirit/the Spirit of Christ—to live within every believer. The body of Christ is a many-membered light of the world, and each of us is a necessary 'little light' in the

Lord's body. We are earthen vessels designed to carry the Light to a broken, bleeding, and dying world.

God's main method of dispelling spiritual darkness in the earth is us. We need to explore the literalness of this fact. When we are in the workplace, the grocery store, or in other common settings, we are like flashlights walking into a cave. Even if we don't say or do anything 'spiritual,' we bring the entrance of light into each and every situation we encounter.

Matthew 5:15–16 indicates that we can hide our light, or in other words, not allow it to shine. Traditionally, we have thought that hiding our light is not telling others about Jesus or not doing good works. The problem that can arise from this mind-set is an overemphasis on 'doing' something in contrast to 'being' in Jesus. We must remember that it is Jesus in us Who is the Light. We cannot produce light but can only let the Light shine from within. If we stress doing good works, as opposed to allowing Christ to live through us, we are in danger of representing Him with deeds done in the flesh. Anything conceived from self-effort will not stand before the "righteous judgment" (John 7:24) of Christ and will burn as wood, hay, and straw (1 Corinthians 3:11–13).

The story of Gideon in Judges 7:15–25 shows us how Jesus—Who is the Light—works in our lives. Gideon was instructed by God to have each of his three-hundred men hold a torch (with a clay pitcher covering the torch) in their left hand. In their right hand, they were to hold a trumpet. Their instructions were to position themselves around the enemy camp and to blow their trumpets and break their pitchers when they heard Gideon blow his trumpet.

When the cue was given, the men did exactly as they were told. Simultaneously, all three hundred men broke their pitchers and blew their trumpets. The result of this obedience to the Lord was the enemy forces attacking themselves with their own swords and fleeing in confusion. The torches represent Jesus, who is the Light. The clay pitchers represent us. We are "earthen vessels" who carry the "treasure" within us.

> But we have this treasure in earthen vessels, so that the surpassing greatness of the power will be of God and not from ourselves. (2 Corinthians 4:7)

The enemy was supernaturally defeated without any other effort on the part of Gideon's army—simply by the light of the torch being exposed. In order to be the light of the world, we must become this spiritual type.

If we yield our will to accept the carefully orchestrated events God has planned or has allowed in our lives, our outer man will begin to crack. As we allow ourselves to be broken, we will be like a city set on a hill and our light will not be able to be hidden. When our earthen vessel is broken, light automatically/naturally (from our nature) will come forth. During this breaking process, we need to remember the joy that is set before us.

> Fixing our eyes on Jesus, the author and perfecter of faith,
> Who for the joy set before Him endured the cross, despising
> the shame, and has sat down at the right hand of the throne of
> God. (Hebrews 12:2)

When we begin to see resurrection life come forth from our earthen vessels—like the light of the torches being released from the broken pitchers—it will be worth it all. Death is not pleasant. Resurrection life/abundant life, however, is on the other side of the grave. In order to be vessels fit for the Master's use, we must choose to "die daily" to our own will and ways.

> Now in a large house there are not only gold and silver vessels,
> but also vessels of wood and of earthenware, and some to honor
> and some to dishonor. (2 Timothy 2:20)

> I affirm, brethren, by the boasting in you which I have in Christ
> Jesus our Lord, I die daily. (1 Corinthians 15:31)

This dying is not 'crucifying ourselves,' for we were crucified with Christ when we were born again. Yet, we are called to give up the right to run our own lives. For the apostle Paul, who penned 1 Corinthians 15:31, dying "daily" meant accepting the continual possibility of physical hardship and death.

The Love of the World

Earlier in this chapter, we looked at Matthew 4:12–17. In this text, Jesus' presence in the lands of Zebulun and Naphtali was compared to the dawning of light. At this time, Jesus proclaimed to the people of Galilee, "Repent, for the Kingdom of Heaven is at hand." The word "repent" means to turn around and go in the other direction or to change your mind. In this application, Jesus was exhorting them to turn from the darkness and to turn to the light.

Regretfully, most people—even Christians—do not want to turn from the darkness to the light. We allow ourselves to become friends with the world and to love what unbelievers love.

> Do not love the world nor the things in the world. If anyone loves the world, the love of the Father is not in him. (1 John 2:15)

In contrast to not being conformed to this world by the renewing of our minds (Romans 12:2), we watch, think, and speak much like the world around us. In the Old Testament story of Lot and his family's escape from the city of Sodom, Lot's wife was turned into a pillar of salt. In disobedience to God's command, she looked back at the city of Sodom. Actually, from the text, I would imagine Lot had to practically drag her out of the city. Despite the impending doom of Sodom, she had so grown to love the things of this world, she could not bring herself to leave a city sentenced to destruction. As she gazed back on the lifestyle she loved, the condition of her heart was revealed. In judgment, God turned her into a pillar of salt—a monument for generations to come as to the danger of loving this world. Sodom was so wicked, God could not allow it to exist. Yet, this daughter of Abraham had so identified with its inhabitants, she could not separate herself from them.

Regretfully, this is the condition of many Christians today. They identify with the darkness in society rather than with the Light. The Lord is currently crying out for repentance from lukewarm Christianity and a turn to the fullness of His kingdom. The majority of the body of Christ is not experiencing the Kingdom of Heaven on earth because they love the darkness rather than the light.

> So Jesus said to them, You will have the Light only a little while longer. Walk while you have the Light [keep on living by it], so that darkness may not overtake and overcome you. He who walks about in the dark does not know where he goes [he is drifting]. While you have the Light, believe in the Light [have faith in it, hold to it, rely on it], that you may become sons of the Light and be filled with Light. Jesus said these things, and then He went away and hid Himself from them [was lost to their view]. (John 12:35–36, AMPC)

Living in the light is a progressive state that will fluctuate continually until we receive our glorified bodies, at which time we will be a full expression of the Light. The gospel of John warns us to live by the light or to live in obedience to God's known will for our lives so that we are not "overcome" by darkness. This means we must continually "press toward the mark for the prize of the high calling of God in Christ Jesus" (Philippians 3:14, KJV) that darkness might not take back lost ground.

Since walking in darkness—for a Christian—is synonymous with walking after the flesh, continuing along the path of darkness will eventually cause us to drift. Soon we will no longer be on the narrow path but will be double-minded and unstable in all our ways (James 1:8). Flirting with darkness is very dangerous and should never be considered innocent or acceptable—even for what we might consider a very short period of time.

John 12:36 speaks of Jesus hiding Himself from them. Although God is omnipresent and Jesus will never leave us or forsake us, this verse is speaking of a distinct time of visitation. There are special seasons in our lives when God draws us to Himself with greater intensity. During these times, He makes His manifest presence more apparent and challenges us to respond to His Spirit in particular areas of our lives. These distinct opportunities to respond to Him are not always available. This has no relevance to our salvation, but the light that shines forth from our lives is in direct proportion to the depth of our intimacy with the Savior.

Our only hope for experiencing the Kingdom of Heaven on this earth is by living in and through the Light. The only hope of the Kingdom of Heaven coming and God's will being done on earth is through the light that shines from our lives. May it never be said of us "that the Light is come into the world, and men loved the darkness rather than the Light; for their deeds were evil" (John 3:19). Amen!

CHAPTER 6

The Beatitudes:
What Kingdom Life Looks Like
Blessed Are the Poor in Spirit

We briefly touched on the necessity of being broken vessels in the last chapter. For Jesus to be seen in us and for His life to be released, our outer man must be broken. The Lord describes the one whose outer man has been broken as being "poor in spirit" or having a "contrite heart."

In Isaiah 57, God describes how He abides with the contrite in heart.

> And it will be said, "Build up, build up, prepare the way, remove every obstacle out of the way of My people." For thus says the high and exalted One Who lives forever, whose name is Holy, "I dwell on a high and holy place, and also with the contrite and lowly of spirit in order to revive the spirit of the lowly and to revive the heart of the contrite." (Isaiah 57:14–15)

A contrite heart gets God's attention.

> For the eyes of the LORD move to and fro throughout the earth
> that He may strongly support those whose heart is completely
> His. (2 Chronicles 16:9a)

Pride is our worst enemy. It was the cause of Lucifer's fall—a passion so strong Lucifer rose up against the God Whom he worshipped day and night. Pride can drive us to entertain thoughts we would never even think in our 'right mind' and to make choices totally out of character. We know the opposite of pride is humility, but we often miss the necessity of the brokenness that precedes humility. Our Heavenly Father breaks our outer man through a series of carefully planned events in our lives. These events are designed to drain us of our self-confidence and bring us to the place of total dependence on God. "Poor in spirit" is the state of a total lack of confidence in our own ability, apart from the out-working of Christ's life within us.

Without brokenness, we will forever be in bondage to self-centeredness. Self-centeredness keeps us from experiencing the abundant life Jesus died to give us. Abundant life is synonymous with Canaan land, or the land of promise, and is God's desire for every one of His children. God brought the nation of Israel out of Egypt with the intention of bringing them into the Promised Land. Similarly, He delivered us from the lineage of Adam and placed us into Christ's lifeline, which is abundant life.

> The thief comes only to steal and kill and destroy; I came that
> they may have life, and have it abundantly. (John 10:10)

Self-centeredness will also keep us from becoming a "vessel for honor, sanctified, useful to the Master" (2 Timothy 2:21). If we fail to choose to overcome in the everyday events of life—which are designed to prepare us for our Master's use—we will fall short of the glory of God. We were specifically designed in our mother's womb, by our Heavenly Father, for the destiny He has for each and every one of us, but the choice to overcome is ours.

In America, there are many ways to escape from the fire God allows or arranges to break our outer man. I call these 'fire escapes.' When the pain of "the fellowship of His sufferings" intensifies, our self-preservation instinct will do all it can to alleviate the pain. Few will ever choose to remain in the fire long enough for their outer man to crack.

> That I may know Him and the power of His resurrection and the fellowship of His sufferings, being conformed to His death. (Philippians 3:10)

We can lead a life of faithful Christian service and have a successful ministry in the power of our flesh and never know "the power of His resurrection." Since the heart of flesh is deceitful, we may not even realize the motives of our hearts until our spiritual eyes are opened through suffering and resultant brokenness.

> The heart is more deceitful than all else and is desperately sick; Who can understand it? (Jeremiah 17:9)

Our Heavenly Father will never leave us in the fire longer than is necessary to set us free from ourselves—we are our own worst enemy! Nonetheless, suffering past the point we can bear in our own strength is necessary, or we will never be broken. We must persevere under trial until we despair of our own strength and choose to rely on His.

Isaiah 57 states that God dwells "with the contrite and lowly of spirit in order to revive the spirit of the lowly and to revive the heart of the contrite." When the Lord's work of redemption in a particular area of our lives is accomplished, He will bring a season of refreshing and revive our spirits and restore our souls. As God works toward preparing us for sonship, it is important to learn to not dread the next step in the refining process. We must learn to relax and enjoy the times of refreshing. As we yield to the processing of the Lord, the joy of freedom from what once had us bound will comfort us through the pain involved in dying to our self-life. Death is the only way to glory!

Through brokenness we are "conformed to His death," and out of death comes resurrection life—new life! Total dependence on the Lord lets us walk through the successive trials of life on this earth with a "quietness" and "confidence" that is truly supernatural. This supernatural "quietness" and "confidence" is our prize for choosing to remain in "the fellowship of His sufferings" until His work is done.

> For thus saith the Lord GOD, the Holy One of Israel; In returning and rest shall ye be saved; in quietness and in confidence shall be your strength. (Isaiah 30:15a, KJV)

This is the strength spoken of in Isaiah 40.

> Yet those who wait for the LORD will gain new strength; They will mount up with wings like eagles, They will run and not get tired, They will walk and not become weary. (Isaiah 40:31)

> When Isaiah spoke prophetically of, "In returning and rest shall ye be saved," the word of the Lord was referring to the availability of entering the "Sabbath rest." When scripture speaks of the "Sabbath rest," it is referring to ceasing from our own works (Hebrews 4:9–10).

When the Lord's work of brokenness brings us to the acknowledgment of our inability to accomplish anything in our own strength, we begin to be "saved" from ourselves. This "saved" is as in "work out your salvation with fear and trembling" (Philippians 2:12). This process of maturity results in "quietness and confidence"—not in ourselves, but in our Lord. Christ, Himself, was the picture for us of "quietness," "confidence," and a contrite heart.

> Let this same attitude and purpose and [humble] mind be in you which was in Christ Jesus: [Let Him be your example in humility:] Who, although being essentially one with God and in the form of God [possessing the fullness of the attributes which make God God], did not think this equality with God

was a thing to be eagerly grasped or retained, But stripped Himself [of all privileges and rightful dignity], so as to assume the guise of a servant [slave], in that He became like men and was born a human being. And after He had appeared in human form, He abased and humbled Himself [still further] and carried His obedience to the extreme of death, even the death of the cross! (Philippians 2:5–8, AMPC)

The prerequisite to a contrite heart—which is referred to as "poor in spirit" in the Beatitudes—is brokenness. The Beatitudes are a list of what we will be like as we walk in the Kingdom of Heaven on earth.

He opened His mouth and began to teach them saying, "Blessed are the poor in spirit, for theirs is the Kingdom of Heaven." (Matthew 5:3)

Poor in Spirit

For our study, it is important to determine whether "poor in spirit" in Matthew 5:3 is referring to our soul or spirit. The Greek word for "spirit" is *"pnuema,"* which is translated as wind, breath, the Holy Spirit and in numerous other ways. Consequently, the original word itself will not shed light on what Matthew was referring to when he said "poor in spirit." However, a consideration of what takes place in our inner man when we are born again will help illuminate this phrase.

When we receive Jesus as our Savior, we become one with Him. Since there is no time or distance in the spirit realm, when He died, we died. Therefore, our old man was crucified with Him, even though Jesus died approximately two thousand years ago. Our death with Him allowed us to be raised to newness of life, which gave us a new nature, which is the nature of Christ. Scripture also tells us that our spirit was made alive through His Spirit. This means the Holy Spirit joined our human spirit. We are now one spirit with the Spirit

94

of the Lord, and our human spirit is no longer distinguishable from the Holy Spirit within us.

Some teach that our human spirit, rather than our nature, is the new-creation part of us. This would replace the human spirit with the Holy Spirit eliminating the human spirit. The problem with this interpretation is that the bible still refers to the human spirit in conjunction with a believer's soul and body. We will take the position then that our inner man consists of our new nature (Christ), our human spirit, and the Holy Spirit. They are all one spirit, even as God the Father, God the Son, and God the Holy Spirit are one. Nevertheless, for the sake of understanding, we will consider the inner man of the believer made up of these three components.

We have reviewed all this to come to the conclusion that if our human spirit, the Holy Spirit and our new nature—which is Jesus—are one, then our inner man is going to choose according to the will of God. In which case, the part of us that will have to be broken of its independence from God is our will, which is a part of our soul. Accordingly, in the context of Matthew 5:3, we will consider being "poor in spirit" as the state of having a broken will.

An End to Self-Effort

One comment in the *Vine's Expository Dictionary* under "poor" gives great insight as to our need to come to the end of any dependence on self-effort. It is noted there, "The poor are constantly the subjects of injunctions to assist them." When we become poor in spirit, we will walk in a constant attitude of need—our need for the grace of God.

In the book of the Song of Solomon, the bride—in her more mature stage of spiritual development—is seen coming out of the wilderness leaning on her beloved. At this place in her spiritual growth, the picture is that she is so dependent on her Lord that she is unable to even sit up by herself. Obviously, most of us are able to sit up on our own, but this represents the bride's heart-attitude of the inability to do anything without Him. "For in Him we live and move and exist" (Acts 17:28a). This is the state of dependence expressed by our Lord when, in reference to His Heavenly Father, He declared, "I can do nothing on My own initiative. As I hear, I judge; and My judgment is just, because I do not seek My own will, but the will of Him who sent Me" (John 5:30).

If we could begin to be the embodiment of the scriptural truth that Jesus is our life, the Kingdom of God would (at the least) be in sight. Similar to the parable of Jesus being the vine and the branches representing us, there is no life in the branches unless it comes through the vine. If we are not depending on the true life within us, we really do not have life but only have existence. When we come to the place where this is no longer head knowledge, we will be nearing the condition that Matthew describes as "poor in spirit."

A Broken Spirit and Contrite Heart

The psalmist spoke of "a broken and contrite heart" as a precious sacrifice to the Lord.

> The sacrifices of God are a broken spirit; A broken and a contrite heart, O God, Thou will not despise. (Psalm 51:17)

As a point of clarification, there is the condition of being brokenhearted from the pain and sorrows of this life. These afflictions were bore by our Lord in His body on the cross, and He longs for us to be free from all of our emotional wounds. This, however, is not the necessary brokenness of self-will that we are referring to as "poor in spirit."

The contrite heart is like the vial of perfume that Mary of Bethany broke and poured over her Lord's head. This was a sacrifice of great value just for the love of her Master. Our lives must also be broken and spilled out as a love offering to our Lord. When something is spilled, it is not confined or limited. We, too, cannot limit what we will allow the Lord to do with our lives. When our will is broken, our limitations of how, when, and where we will be used— and our demands on God—are left at the altar.

What It Means to Be Blessed

The next concept we need to understand in our title passage is what it means to be "blessed." According to *Tenney's Dictionary of the Bible*, to be blessed means "a declaration of blessedness or the joys of heaven." A declaration of blessedness seems redundant, but the thought of the joys of heaven is one we can grasp. According to this definition, to be blessed is to experience the joys of heaven on earth.

The *Amplified Bible* gives some powerful descriptions of being "blessed." One synonym for being blessed is "happy, to be envied" (Matthew 5:3, AMPC). Can you imagine being so happy you would be the envy of those around you? At this time, probably few of us fit into this category. Yet, Jesus is saying this is the inheritance of the poor in spirit. Another description of being "blessed" is to be "spiritually prosperous." To be spiritually prosperous is to find favor with both God and man.

The psalmist describes this state of spiritual prosperity as being "like a tree firmly planted by streams of water, which yields its fruit in its season, and its leaf does not wither; and in whatever he does he prospers" (Psalm 1:3). The spiritually prosperous will not grow weary in well-doing. They are steadfast and faithful because they draw on the limitless resources of the life of Christ within them. He is a river of living water that flows from the throne of God through each and every believer. The "prosperous" one knows how to draw all he needs, for every moment of every day, from the Living Water. This is a major attribute of kingdom life.

Yet another description of "blessed" from the *Amplified Bible* is, "With life-joy and satisfaction in God's favor and salvation, regardless of their outward condition." When our lives start to be an outward expression of this definition of blessed, the world will want to know our Jesus.

The life of the apostle Paul was a pattern of a life that suffered many afflictions. He was persecuted, shipwrecked, stoned, left as dead, and more, and yet in Philippians chapter 4, he said, "Not that I speak from want; for I have learned to be content in whatever circumstances I am. I know how to get along with humble means, and

I also know how to live in prosperity; in any and every circumstance I have learned the secret of being filled and going hungry, both of having abundance and suffering need. I can do all things through Him who strengthens me" (Philippians 4:11–15).

Joy and satisfaction, regardless of our outward circumstances, is truly a supernatural quality. Since the supernatural life of God dwells within us, we should expect supernatural fruit in our lives! The secret to experiencing the kind of contentment the apostle Paul displayed is to be poor in spirit. Then, along with Paul, we will be able to share from our own experience, "In everything give thanks; for this is God's will for you in Christ Jesus" (1 Thessalonians 5:18).

The Power of Grace

The last facet of the word "blessed" from the *Amplified Bible* is, "A happiness from the revelation of His matchless grace." To be blessed means to have great happiness solely from an understanding of the grace of God. The word "grace" comes from the Greek word *"charis,"* which is defined by *Strong's Hebrew and Greek Dictionary* as "the divine influence upon the heart and its reflection in the life." The Holy Spirit—through a power beyond ourselves—influences our wills and transforms our minds to conform us into an expression of our Heavenly Father in the earth.

Although we can choose our own way and choose to be disobedient and walk after the flesh, to do so we have to struggle against the power of the Holy Spirit. In contrast to disobedience, for those who have trained themselves to be continually dependent on the grace of God, His "grace is sufficient" for every need. When we depend on His grace, His power supernaturally changes us into the image of Christ.

And He has said to me, "My grace is sufficient for you, for power is perfected in weakness." Most gladly, therefore, I will rather boast about my weaknesses, so that the power of Christ may dwell in me. (2 Corinthians 12:9)

A common definition of grace is, "unmerited favor." Through absolutely nothing we have done or could ever do, God has forgiven all our sin through the sacrifice of His Son. We have become partakers of His divine nature through His Spirit, Who lives within us (2 Peter 1:4). His nature has also made us righteous—despite all we have ever thought, said, or done. The brokenness that precedes being "poor in spirit" results in a deep knowledge that there is nothing we can do of ourselves and that God is in total control. Nothing will ever touch us that our loving Father has not allowed. This revelation of our need for His matchless grace results in unspeakable joy and great rest, since we know all we will ever need has already been supplied through Him.

Another definition of grace is, "the power and desire to do God's will." The grace of God gives us the ability and even the desire to be obedient to the known will of God. Our Heavenly Father sent His Son to give us everything we need for life and godliness. He did not give us an instruction book—the Bible—for the purpose of discouraging us with our lack of success. Moreover, He sent His Holy Spirit as the administrator of His grace so that all things written might be possible through Christ Jesus. This alone should be enough to give us great joy.

The more we walk with the broken and contrite heart of the poor in spirit, the more we will access the unlimited resources of His grace. As a result of this chosen dependence on God, we will experience ever-increasing joy as we see His supernatural enabling in our everyday lives.

The last—but very important—definition of grace is, "His ability for our inability." In other words, in every situation in life where we are lacking in patience, peace, understanding, or anything else imaginable—whether of mind, will, emotion, spirit, soul, or body—the grace of God is available to replace our inability with His ability. If we could realize how literal this promise is, we could be spared much sorrow and hardship in this life. Our Lord is just waiting for us to ask for His ability, which He desires to lavish freely upon us.

Therefore let us draw near with confidence to the throne of grace, so that we may receive mercy and find grace to help in time of need. (Hebrews 4:16)

Part of the reason we do not run to the throne of grace for every need is because our mortal minds cannot even begin to comprehend all the Lord desires to do for us. The apostle Paul expressed our need for spiritual enlightenment in his letter to the Ephesians.

I pray that the eyes of your heart may be enlightened, so that you will know what is the hope of His calling, what are the riches of the glory of His inheritance in the saints, and what is the surpassing greatness of His power toward us who believe. These are in accordance with the working of the strength of His might which He brought about in Christ, when He raised Him from the dead and seated Him at His right hand in the heavenly places. (Ephesians 1:18–20)

The more we understand what the Lord has given us, the more we will go to the throne of grace for help with every need. The more we experience the Lord's abundant provision in our time of need, the more our faith will grow. Through this process, we can develop the habit of asking for the grace of the Lord when we begin to struggle— rather than after we fall apart.

Your Life Is Not Your Own

The "poor in spirit" also know they have no rights of their own.

Or do you not know that your body is a temple of the Holy Spirit who is in you, whom you have from God, and that you are not your own? For you have been bought with a price: there- fore glorify God in your body. (1 Corinthians 6:19–20)

It is a very difficult thing to give up all our rights to the discre- tion of the Lord. We must surrender every member of our family, all that we possess, our health and happiness, and all our hopes and dreams. We really have no rights to any of these (even though we live as though we do) because we "are not" our "own."

Our brokenness also allows us to become living sacrifices for the Lord's use. His design has always been to have sons and daughters to share His life with, but until we are broken, we are not available for the Master's use.

> I urge you therefore, brethren, by the mercies of God, to present your bodies a living and holy sacrifice, acceptable to God, which is your spiritual service of worship. (Romans 12:1)

A living sacrifice was an animal brought to the temple as a sacrifice to God. However, instead of killing the animal, the sacrifice was given for the service of the temple—all the days of its life. This is what we are to be if we are to enjoy the blessedness promised to the "poor in spirit." The poor in spirit have retained no rights of their own but are so broken of self-will they have become vessels "for honor, sanctified, useful to the Master, prepared for every good work" (2 Timothy 2:21).

A Resting Place for God

We are the "temple of the Holy Spirit" and the Lord desires to find "rest" within us. God longs to have the fellowship and the cooperative relationship with us we were created for. Yet, this will only be experienced to the degree we have a broken and contrite spirit. We must realize we will never find fulfillment until God's will is accomplished in us.

> Thus says the LORD, "Heaven is My throne and the earth is My footstool. Where then is a house you could build for Me? And where is a place that I may rest? For My hand made all these things, Thus all these things came into being," declares the LORD. "But to this one I will look, To him who is humble and contrite of spirit, and who trembles at My word." (Isaiah 66:1–2)

As "the eyes of the LORD move to and fro throughout the earth," may He find what He is looking for in us—a resting place for Him (2 Chronicles 16:9a)!

CHAPTER 7

The Beatitudes:
What Kingdom Life Looks Like
Blessed Are Those Who Mourn

Blessed are those who mourn, for they shall be comforted.
—Matthew 5:4

Upon the birthing of His earthly ministry, Jesus spent time in the synagogues teaching the religious people of His day what the Kingdom of Heaven was really like. One of His first announcements was that through His incarnation, the Kingdom of God had come to earth. This kind of talk infuriated the religious leaders, as He taught of a present kingdom—invisible to the natural eye and accessible only through Him. His teaching was not only contrary to their traditions but was the opposite of what they expected the Kingdom of Heaven to be like.

In this Beatitude, Jesus made one of His first hard-to-understand statements. He declared the blessedness of mourning, which we typically associate with funerals, death, and loss! Nonetheless, "True joy must necessarily be the fruit of sorrow."[6] We must have need in order to know the joy of the fulfillment of that need. Throughout

---

[6] Clarke's Commentary on the Bible, e-sword

scripture, we see similar seemingly contradictory statements, such as the need to be emptied before we can be filled, to be weak before we can be strong, and to be last in order to be first. The grace of God always flows into our need, not our sufficiency.

This principle also holds true with mourning. The very desperateness of our need prepares and expands a place in our hearts for the healing grace of God to fill with joy. Accordingly, this is true joy since the 'real thing' cannot be duplicated but is a fruit of, or a result of, the Holy Spirit in our lives. Any substitute for joy the world or the flesh may offer is not of the same character or quality and will fail us during times of testing. The joy that springs from our innermost being during times of need is far greater than anything we can ever experience from any other source.

Paradoxically, it is often difficult for us to be willing to undergo the painful experiences of life, which are necessary for the grace of God we really long for. In fact, it is the intensity of the experience itself that brings us to the point of desperation, which compels us to finally let go of what we are clinging to, in order to receive the abundance of God's provision and grace. In the journal of martyred missionary Jim Elliot, these immortal words were penned: "He is no fool who gives what he cannot keep, to gain what he cannot lose."

In the context of mourning, we must be willing to walk through times of great sorrow in order to experience the joy and the depth of relationship the Lord desires. It is His desire to give us His best, when we would tend to be content with less, rather than experience the pain and sorrow of restraint. In *Come Away My Beloved*, written as from the Lord Himself, the late Frances J. Roberts penned these words:

> My child, I am coming to you walking upon the waters of the sorrows of your life; even above the sounds of the storm you will hear My voice calling your name. You are never alone, for I am at your right hand. Never despair, for I am watching over and caring for you. Do not be anxious. What presently seems to be a difficult situation to you is all part of My planning, and I am working out the details

of circumstances to the end that I may bless you and reveal Myself to you in a new way.

As I have opened your eyes to see, so I will open your ears to hear, and you will come to know Me even as Moses did, in a face-to-face relationship. For I will remove the veil that separates Me from you and you will know Me as your dearest Friend and as your truest Comforter (updated by author).[7]

This "face-to-face relationship" many desire comes through repeated, seemingly unbearable circumstances through which the Lord reveals Himself to us—"walking upon the waters of the sorrows" of our lives. The storms of life allow our Beloved to reveal Himself to us in ways we would never know without the intensity of the storm.

Isaiah 61 encourages us to press through our times of mourning for the rewards waiting for us on the other side.

> The Spirit of the Lord GOD is upon me, Because the LORD has anointed me To bring good news to the afflicted; He has sent me to bind up the brokenhearted, To proclaim liberty to captives And freedom to prisoners; To proclaim the favorable year of the LORD And the day of vengeance of our God; To comfort all who mourn, To grant those who mourn in Zion, Giving them a garland instead of ashes, The oil of gladness instead of mourning, The mantle of praise instead of a spirit of fainting. So they will be called oaks of righteousness, The planting of the LORD, that He may be glorified. (Isaiah 61:1–3)

From this text in Isaiah, we see the Father has great concern for us when we are brokenhearted. In fact, two of the great burdens Christ bore in His body on the cross were our "grief" and "sorrows."

[7.] "Come Away My Beloved," Frances J. Roberts, page 16, *On the Waters of Sorrow*

Surely our griefs He Himself bore, And our sorrows He carried;
Yet we ourselves esteemed Him stricken, Smitten of God, and
afflicted. (Isaiah 53:4)

In Isaiah 61:1, we are told that Jehovah "anointed" Jesus "to
bind up the brokenhearted." A basic definition of "anointed" is
God's assignment of, or the presence of the Holy Spirit in order to
accomplish a God-ordained destiny or task. This enabling by the
Holy Spirit to do God's will is limitless. We tend to think of anointing as only for spiritual endeavors, but in reality, anointing can be
given for any task in life. This text from Isaiah shows that our Father
so desires for us to experience abundant life, that He placed a special
empowering of the Holy Spirit upon Jesus for the healing of the
brokenhearted.

Isaiah 61 relates that the heart of God is "to comfort all who
mourn." The good news of the gospel is proclaimed specifically for
those who mourn. The Lord promises a "garland instead of ashes."
The King James Version's rendering of "garland" in this verse is
"beauty." In other words, the Lord desires to transform the times we
have mourned 'in sackcloth and ashes' to beautiful monuments of
His love, constant care, and provision.

It also is His will to give us "the oil of gladness instead of
mourning." The "oil" speaks figuratively of riches and fruitful-
ness—to replace our poverty and barrenness. It speaks spiritually of
the presence of the Holy Spirit 'oozing' out of our brokenness and
bringing forth the character of Christ in the very places of our worst
memories. In fact, we can be so changed through our experiences of
grief and sorrow we can learn to thank the Lord for everything, since
nothing touches us apart from the lifting of His hand. The lips that
cried continually to the Lord for the strength to even make it from
day to day will be able to praise the Lord for His amazing deliverance
when there seemed to be no hope. The end result of the situation
that, at times, made us despair of life, will be that we have been made
"strong in the Lord, and in the power of his might" (Ephesians 6:10).
We will have become such an expression of the Lord in the earth,

we "will be called oaks of righteousness," and our lives will unconsciously give Him glory.

Expect and Embrace Tribulation!

Scripture clearly teaches us to expect to mourn and sorrow over trials and tribulations. One of the greatest hazards in the spiritual development of new believers is for Christian leaders and teachers to underplay this truth or to not teach it at all.

For some strange reason—probably wishful thinking—we like to think because we are attempting to follow God and walk in obedience to Him, we should be exempt from the hardships of the world in which we live. Whereas, scripture clearly teaches against this fallacy.

> These things I have spoken to you, that in Me you may have peace. In the world you will have tribulation; but be of good cheer, I have overcome the world. (John 16:33, NKJV)

> But I say to you, love your enemies and pray for those who persecute you, so that you may be sons of your Father who is in heaven; for He causes His sun to rise on the evil and the good, and sends rain on the righteous and the unrighteous. (Matthew 5:44–45)

Tribulation is what forms us into the image of Christ. If we understand God's ways, it is much easier to walk in peace through what, at times, seems like endless trials. If we embrace the unpleasant things in life as from the hand of the Lord, they actually set us free from ourselves. As teachers and leaders, we need to present the thrill of the battle and the assurance of victory in the Lord—possibly not as we expected—but certainly God's "expected end" (Jeremiah 29:11).

In speaking of the necessity of tribulation, A. B. Simpson, a powerful prophet from the late 1800s, wrote:

> Not much longer shall we have glorious opportunity to rejoice in tribulation and learn patience. In heaven we

shall have nothing to teach us long-suffering. If we do not learn it here, we shall be without our brightest crown forever and wish ourselves back for a little while in the very circumstances of which we are now trying so hard to rid ourselves.[8]

Due to the fact that we reap what we sow, we can expect much of what we would consider 'good' from the hand of our Father. However, at the same time, God does not promise to shield us from the hardships of this life but does promise—in a way only He can—that the evil in this world will ultimately result in good for us.

> And we know that God causes all things to work together for good to those who love God, to those who are called according to His purpose. For those whom He foreknew, He also predestined to become conformed to the image of His Son, so that He would be the firstborn among many brethren. (Romans 8:28–29)

No matter how horrendous a situation we walk through may be, if we receive it with thanksgiving, we can experience the Kingdom of God—with all that it holds—in the midst of the storm.

> For the Kingdom of God is not eating and drinking, but righteousness and peace and joy in the Holy Spirit. (Romans 14:17)

Before we were ever born, God's plan for each of us was for us to "become conformed to the image of His Son." With this purpose in mind—no matter what the world or the enemy throws at us—God can use our circumstances as a tool to make us like Him (with our cooperation). Since our Heavenly Father is the Master Craftsman, only He knows what is necessary to bring forth the beautiful masterpiece He is creating. Only He can possibly know what to allow or what to protect us from. Job—as a blameless man in the midst of

---

[8.] *Days of Heaven on Earth*, A.B. Simpson, February 11

unbelievable suffering—spoke words that reveal a deep understanding of God's ways:

> He said, "Naked I came from my mother's womb, And naked I shall return there. The LORD gave and the LORD has taken away. Blessed be the name of the LORD." (Job 1:21)

> "Shall we indeed accept good from God and not accept adversity?" In all this Job did not sin with his lips. (Job 2:10b)

> Though He slay me, yet will I trust Him. (Job 13:15a, NKJV)

Joseph also suffered unimaginable trials that were totally contrary to God's revelation for his life. It was sixteen years before the Lord began to unfold His promised destiny in Joseph's life. Joseph's response to his brothers, whose foul treatment of him had been the beginning of his sixteen years of tribulation, was to acknowledge God's "higher" (Isaiah 55:9) ways.

> As for you, you meant evil against me, but God meant it for good in order to bring about this present result, to preserve many people alive. (Genesis 50:20)

When Shadrach, Meshach, and Abednego were threatened with the fiery furnace for not bowing down to King Nebuchadnezzar's golden image, they boldly declared their confidence in the God of our trials, as well as the God of our comfort.

> If it be so, our God whom we serve is able to deliver us from the furnace of blazing fire; and He will deliver us out of your hand, O king. But even if He does not, let it be known to you, O king, that we are not going to serve your gods or worship the golden image that you have set up. (Daniel 3:17–18)

We can see—without a doubt—that trials and tribulation in this life are a necessary part of our training for eternity and our preparation for the ages to come. In order to be victorious, we must continually keep in mind that the all-powerful God is always with us and in us. If we correctly respond to what the Lord allows as we walk through situations we would not have chosen for ourselves, our mourning will be turned to gladness and we will be anointed with the oil of joy.

God—the Source of Discipline

Not only does God allow trials in our lives, but at times—in the process of conforming us into the image of His Son—He will also be the initiator of these times of testing.

> For consider Him who has endured such hostility by sinners against Himself, so that you will not grow weary and lose heart. You have not yet resisted to the point of shedding blood in your striving against sin; and you have forgotten the exhortation which is addressed to you as sons, "My son, do not regard lightly the discipline of the lord, nor faint when you are reproved by him; for those whom the lord loves he disciplines, and he scourges every son whom he receives." It is for discipline that you endure; God deals with you as with sons; for what son is there whom his father does not discipline? (Hebrews 12:3–7)

I cannot stress enough how important it is for us to understand God's ways and to feel His heart. Much of our emotional distress in a time of trial is due to a misunderstanding of how God works in the midst of His people. It is imperative we lay down our thoughts and expectations as to how we think God should respond in each and every situation and renew our minds with the word of God.

> Therefore I urge you, brethren, by the mercies of God, to present your bodies a living and holy sacrifice, acceptable to God, which is your spiritual service of worship. And do not be conformed to this world, but be transformed by the renewing of

your mind, so that you may prove what the will of God is, that which is good and acceptable and perfect. (Romans 12:1–2)

The first two verses of Hebrews 12 show us the healthy mindset we need in order to "not grow weary and lose heart."

Therefore, since we have so great a cloud of witnesses surrounding us, let us also lay aside every encumbrance and the sin which so easily entangles us, and let us run with endurance the race that is set before us, fixing our eyes on Jesus, the author and perfecter of faith, who for the joy set before Him endured the cross, despising the shame, and has sat down at the right hand of the throne of God. (Hebrews 12:1–2)

During the Church Age, life lived on this earth can be compared to a "race." Our Heavenly Father trains us to have the "endurance" to run the race He has destined for us. Keeping our "eyes on Jesus"—as opposed to the circumstances around us—is the only way for us to finish the race. Since "the cross is the pain involved in doing the will of God,"[9] we are only able to bear the "pain" by setting our minds on "the joy set before" us, so we are not overwhelmed by the emotions of the moment.

Athletes are willing to go through excruciating pain just to excel at a sport that—in the scope of eternity—is only temporary. Many are willing to take great risks and, at times, experience great pain just for the 'thrill' of an extreme sport or for a moment of notoriety. How much more should we be willing to identify with the suffering of our Lord for eternal purposes?

The Fellowship of Suffering

Beloved, do not be surprised at the fiery ordeal among you, which comes upon you for your testing, as though some strange thing were happening to you; but to the degree that you share

---

[9.] _My Utmost for His Highest._ Oswald Chambers

the sufferings of Christ, keep on rejoicing, so that also at the revelation of His glory you may rejoice with exultation. (1 Peter 4:12–13)

Now I rejoice in my sufferings for your sake, and in my flesh I do my share on behalf of His body, which is the church, in filling up what is lacking in Christ's afflictions. (Colossians 1:24)

The glory (character) of God will be revealed through us to "the degree that" we "share the sufferings of Christ." As we see "His appearing" (2 Timothy 4:8) in our lives, we will be able to "rejoice" in the fact that we are not the person we used to be.

That I may know Him and the power of His resurrection and the fellowship of His sufferings, being conformed to His death. (Philippians 3:10)

Therefore, since Christ has suffered in the flesh, arm yourselves also with the same purpose, because he who has suffered in the flesh has ceased from sin, so as to live the rest of the time in the flesh no longer for the lusts of men, but for the will of God. (1 Peter 4:1–2)

God Means What He Says—Take Him Seriously!

There is one more very important "mourning" spoken of in the bible. This is the necessary mourning that results from an awareness and healthy response to our sinful condition. Repentance is often seen as an unpleasant experience, despite the fact that it cleanses us from a deadly condition. Repentance frees us from a state of being that—left unchecked—will, at the best, reap a decline in the quality of our life. At that point, if the spiritual decline is left unchecked, it could lead to the hardening of our hearts and the possibility of the eventual rejection of our need for a savior.

Beyond our own destruction from refusing to repent is the path of destruction we would leave for those who look to us as an example of Christ. We may never realize how many people our lives affect, including many we never knew were watching. In consideration of the best scenario, our lack of repentance will surely tarnish the lives of our loved ones, as well as generations to come. Repentance is as necessary for our spiritual health as medical treatment for a deadly disease is in the natural. However, in the case of repentance, the ramifications of going our own way are far greater. For these reasons the book of James gives a solemn admonition:

> Draw near to God and He will draw near to you. Cleanse your hands, you sinners; and purify your hearts, you double-minded. Be miserable and mourn and weep; let your laughter be turned into mourning and your joy to gloom. (James 4:8–9)

James is exhorting us to pay attention to the prompting of the Holy Spirit. The Holy Spirit was given to us as a friend and a guide. It is foolish to ignore His conviction—continuing on with life as if there aren't any problems between God and ourselves. Since ignoring the Holy Spirit will always lead to a decline in the quality of life and, if left unchecked, eventual destruction, it is without a doubt better to choose to "be miserable and mourn and weep."

Every moment we spend on the path of destruction allows the enemy of our souls to "steal, kill, and destroy" (John 10:10) the good God intends for us. Few would ever desire to go through surgery, but most would rather go through treatment than let a disease go untreated and ravage their bodies. It is crucial to see the effects of sin in our lives and the lives of those around us for what it is! If we have allowed our hearts to be hardened, or if we have become rebellious or unteachable, we need to mourn over our condition. We need to hate "even the garment polluted by the flesh" (Jude 1:23).

In the day in which we live, it is especially essential to walk in close communion with the Lord. Judgment begins in the house of the Lord, and the closer we get to "the marriage supper of the Lamb" (Revelation 19:9), the greater the intensity of the "refiner's fire" (Malachi 3:2). The Lord is presently preparing a people, from among a people, to have a special place in the culmination of all things. He calls this group "sons of God," "overcomers," "the 144,000," and ultimately, "His bride."

The Harvest Is Before Us

The choices you make today will not only determine your destiny in this life but will also have a far-reaching effect on your ranking in the Kingdom of Heaven. If you choose to live a lukewarm life—identifying with the apathetic Laodicean church—you will one day regret your decision. While you wait to die and go to heaven or look to being 'raptured' in your carnality, your decision and your delay in mourning over your spiritual condition will reap eternal consequences. Joel prophetically spoke of this day.

> The LORD utters His voice before His army; Surely His camp is very great, For strong is he who carries out His word. The day of the LORD is indeed great and very awesome, And who can endure it? "Yet even now," declares the LORD, "Return to Me with all your heart, And with fasting, weeping and mourning; And rend your heart and not your garments." (Joel 2:11b–13a)

As crucial as it is for believers to mourn over carnality in their lives, it is equally urgent for unbelievers to see their lost condition. The final harvest of souls from the earth is before us, and the urgency of mourning over the lost condition of our souls now—before it is too late—increases every day. When the Lord finally releases His wrath upon the earth, the people of the world in which we live will mourn, wishing they had repented of their self-centeredness before the return of the Lord. Matthew 24 gives us a picture of this:

> And then the sign of the Son of Man will appear in the sky, and then all the tribes of the earth will mourn, and they will see the son of man coming on the clouds of the sky with power and great glory. (Matthew 24:30)

The Good Side of Mourning

The ultimate truth is, not only is mourning not a bad thing, but it is often very good for us. For with the Lord, the result of "godly sorrow" (2 Corinthians 7:10, KJV) is always better than our former condition. In the text from Isaiah 61, which we previously looked at, the KJV states that God will give us "beauty for ashes." The Lord turns the pain and sorrow of this life, which could cause us to mourn, into ashes.

As we think about "ashes," we know they eventually blow away and are forgotten. They also lose their original shape and cease to be a continual reminder of the past. Remarkably, ashes are even valuable for use as fertilizer. The nitrogen in ashes causes rapid growth in green plants. Since we are the "planting of the Lord" (Isaiah 61:3), He promises that more spiritual growth and strength can come from the very "ashes" of our lives—more than we could ever imagine. As we correctly respond to the circumstances the Lord allows, luscious green growth—beauty—can arise from the midst of a pile of ashes from our lives.

Not only will "those who mourn" be "comforted," but they will also become strong trees undaunted by the worst of life's storms. It has often been said, "No pain, no gain." This is equally true in the Kingdom of God—with the added incentive that our "gain" is eternal.

For all of these reasons, I leave you with a challenge: Never draw back from what the Lord allows in your life. Moreover, I encourage you to ultimately choose to overcome until your "pain" becomes "gain." For "godliness with contentment is great gain" (Titus 6:6)!

CHAPTER 8

The Beatitudes:
What Kingdom Life Looks Like
Blessed Are the Humble

In this chapter, we will be studying humility, which is very similar to being "poor in spirit." The difference is important enough, however, that Jesus taught it as a separate Beatitude. The significant difference between the two is that being "poor in spirit" is the brokenness necessary for the release of the Lord's humility.

Humility is a divine attribute and, as such, is not something we can make happen. The only thing we can do is allow ourselves to be broken and spilled out, in order to make a place for the Lord's humility to come forth.

> Blessed are the gentle, for they shall inherit the earth. (Matthew 5:5)

As previously discussed, "blessed" is defined as having "joy and satisfaction in God's favor and salvation regardless of our outward conditions." We usually think of this Beatitude as it's translated in the King James Version: "Blessed are the meek." The original Greek word in this verse (in both the NASB and KJV) is *"praus,"* which by implication means humble. For this reason, in this chapter we will be looking at the blessedness of humility.

Yoked with the Lord

In recent years, the Lord has given me an understanding of Matthew 11:28–30 that is different from any thoughts I had previously held. In reference to this, one section of scripture may have many implications or facets and may also have many layers of meaning. In no way does this take away from the accuracy of scripture, but it does speak of the wisdom of God and the part the Holy Spirit plays in making the written word (the bible) alive and applicable to every age and every situation. The word of God is alive, and we will never totally understand it or get bored due to the Holy Spirit's ever-changing enlightenment of the never-changing word.

> Come to Me, all who are weary and heavy-laden, and I will give you rest. Take My yoke upon you and learn from Me, for I am gentle and humble in heart, and you will find rest for your souls. For My yoke is easy and My burden is light. (Matthew 11:28–30)

This passage has typically been used to show unbelievers the benefits of coming to the Lord. Although this certainly is an invitation to unbelievers, it is also an encouragement to all who are "weary and heavy-laden." The depth of our rest in the Lord is a barometer of our spiritual maturity. Hence, this verse is an invitation for rest to all believers, at any place in their spiritual growth, as well as to unbelievers.

We have already studied the Sabbath rest in previous chapters, but since the Sabbath rest is the goal of our Christian walk and is synonymous with Christlikeness, it will be a much-repeated phrase throughout this book. We see in this passage, if we would put the Lord's yoke upon us, we would find rest for our souls. This rest is the Sabbath rest and will continue to be a greater reality in our lives in direct proportion to our spiritual growth. In other words, our level of rest or spiritual maturity will be in direct correlation to the Lord's yoke being upon us.

The Lord's yoke refers to our availability of being used as an expression of His life in the earth. As we saw in the last chapter, being "poor in spirit" is the heart-attitude that allows us to be used by the Lord. The other aspect of His yoke is an unreserved commitment to being obedient to His known will for our lives. We may also think of His yoke as the "cross" He asks us to bear. The late Oswald Chambers made taking up our "cross" practical when he taught, "The cross is the pain involved in doing the will of God."

> And He was saying to them all, "If anyone wishes to come after Me, he must deny himself, and take up his cross daily and follow Me. (Luke 9:23)

If we are yoked with the Lord, following Him will be automatic. To 'follow' Him will require such a natural (according to our nature) obedience it will be as if we are connected to Him with a literal wooden yoke. At this level of surrender—even in the painful places of life—the union that began with new birth will become an ever-increasing reality until we become like Him—spirit, soul, and body.

> Now may the God of peace Himself sanctify you entirely; and may your spirit and soul and body be preserved complete, without blame at the coming of our Lord Jesus Christ. (1 Thessalonians 5:23)

We have seen that taking the Lord's yoke upon us will lead to Sabbath rest and will result in union with Him. Further down in our text from Matthew 11, we see that taking His yoke upon us will also mean we will "learn" of Him—that He is "gentle and humble in heart." If we learn from His example and see our need for gentleness and humility, His yoke can be "easy" and His "burden" can be "light."

Once again, we cannot change ourselves. However, if we sincerely ask God to give us the grace of gentleness and humility, He will be faithful to give His "sufficient" grace (2 Corinthians 12:9).

Notwithstanding, we must remember the Lord's character typically only becomes ours as we walk through circumstances that force us to rely on His power to overcome.

In conclusion, in order to find rest for our souls and for the Lord's "yoke" to be "easy" and His "burden" to be "light," we must be "gentle and humble in heart." If the yoke of the Lord seems too heavy to us, a possible reason could be our pride and the resulting demand for our rights. Our own pride is a heavy weight that will rob us of peace, joy, life, and vitality. We rarely know how proud we actually are until the Lord shines His light on what is really in our hearts. The startling fact is that our hearts of flesh are "deceitful" and "desperately wicked" (Jeremiah 17:9, NKJV), and we don't even know what we are really like.

Pride—One of Satan's Most Used Weapons

One of the greatest weapons Satan uses to destroy Christians is pride. Our pride will also be a continual hindrance to our spiritual growth and a barrier between the Lord and us.

> But He gives a greater grace. Therefore it says, "God is opposed to the proud, but gives grace to the humble." (James 4:6)

The book of James records a very simple principle: If we are humble, dependence on God will be our heart's natural position. We will boldly go to "the throne of grace," and we will find "help" for every "need."

> Therefore let us draw near with confidence to the throne of grace, so that we may receive mercy and find grace to help in time of need. (Hebrews 4:16)

The opposite is also true. If we are proud—in keeping with His own word—God has to oppose us. Forcing God to oppose us due to our rebellion and independence is a scary thought. Even if our pride doesn't force the Lord to oppose us, in the very best scenario, we would still not be recipients of His grace. Without grace—with all of its definitions—we are destined for spiritual defeat.

Religious pride can be the most deadly type of pride and is the most subtle to detect. It is very possible for us to observe the spiritual disciplines of a committed Christian only to become proud of our performance. There is an extreme danger from this form of pride. If we continue to embrace our haughty thoughts, rather than taking them to the cross, our flesh is an open door to a religious or antichrist spirit, which is deadly to us and to the work of the Lord.

> For by the grace [unmerited favor of God] given to me I warn everyone among you not to estimate and think of himself more highly than he ought [not to have an exaggerated opinion of his own importance], but to rate his ability with sober judgment, each according to the degree of faith apportioned by God to him. (Romans 12:3, AMPC)

It is so easy to forget the only reason we are even able to please the Lord is because of the life of Christ within us—applied to our lives by the Holy Spirit—which was freely given to us by "grace [unmerited favor of God]." Even if we believe we are where we are at in our walk with the Lord because of our faith, the word is clear that we possess "the degree of faith apportioned" to us "by God." We need to fear spiritual pride like a plague—because it is! It is a deadly virus that moves unseen throughout the body of Christ, causing weakness in the body and even spiritual death for those who are deceived by it!

The only way to conquer spiritual pride is to confront it as soon as we feel it rising up in our hearts. We must immediately ask the Lord for the grace of humility and apply the work of the cross to our flesh. Since spiritual pride is a deed of the flesh and is a carry-over from our old man, by faith we must "consider" ourselves "dead to sin" (Romans 6:11). The application of our co-crucifixion with Christ is powerful in the battle against our flesh.

Another symptom of spiritual pride is taking credit for whatever success we may have in life—forgetting where we would have been without the Lord. Even if our life is relatively stable and 'successful,' it was the grace of God that either allowed us to have the family and heritage we have or that gave us the power to overcome a hard beginning in life.

Many who were delivered from much bondage when they came to the Lord have a tendency to be spiritually proud toward those who are suffering from the same family history and bondage they were delivered from. Scripture warns us that we judge others in the things we have a tendency to do ourselves (or would still do apart from the Lord).

> Therefore you have no excuse, every one of you who passes judgment, for in that which you judge another, you condemn yourself; for you who judge practice the same things. (Romans 2:1)

Self-righteousness sees the Christian walk as a ladder and each rung as a spiritual discipline or a self-sacrifice we feel makes us acceptable or loved by God. It is not that our rungs are 'bad' in themselves, but we can have carnal motivation behind our performance. If we are driven to achieve these rungs for our spiritual self-esteem, spiritual pride is the condition of our hearts and, as a result, our spiritual disciplines can be works of the flesh. In contrast, if we are secure in God's total love and acceptance of us because we are "in Christ," our works are an outflow of His life and love and are fueled by grace. These are works that remain.

> Each man's work will become evident; for the day will show it because it is to be revealed with fire, and the fire itself will test the quality of each man's work. (1 Corinthians 3:13)

There is great potential danger to the body of Christ from self-righteousness. When we base our acceptance from the Lord on the steps in our 'ladder,' the tendency is to cast stones at anyone who has different rungs on their ladder or to blast those who can't keep up with our achievements. As a result of our pride, we actually destroy other members of our own "body," instead of extending the grace and mercy God has extended to us. It is most probable, if we are not kind and merciful, as our Father is merciful (Luke 6:36), deep in our hearts we really don't believe we are where we are only by the grace of God!

> Be of the same mind toward one another; do not be haughty in mind, but associate with the lowly. Do not be wise in your own estimation. (Romans 12:16)

> Let nothing be done through selfish ambition or conceit, but in lowliness of mind let each esteem others better than himself. (Philippians 2:3, NKJV)

When the Lord began speaking to me about Philippians 2:3, I had a hard time understanding how we could honestly always "esteem others better than" ourselves. Since the Lord has deposited different gifts and talents in each of us, it is to be expected that the person with a gift or talent I do not have is going to be better at that discipline than I am. Conversely, if I have a gift in a certain area, how could I possibly consider someone else "better than" myself when God did not intend for him or her to be able to excel in that area?

As I talked to the Lord about this, I heard a teaching that finally gave me an understanding of this verse—one that set well with my heart. If we use the relationship between a master and a slave as an example, most would consider the master—as the one being served— to be of more importance than the slave, who is the servant. Thus, esteeming others better than ourselves is not a matter of comparing their performance with ours but is a conscious choice to honor them above ourselves. Therefore, we "esteem others better than" ourselves by serving them with "lowliness of mind."

God Must Oppose the Proud

Let's switch our train of thought to an Old Testament account of how God worked humility in a very proud king. In Daniel chapter 4, God gives King Nebuchadnezzar a vision of the king's impending judgment. The king calls for Daniel to give him the interpretation of his vision. Although the interpretation reveals God's judgment upon the king, Daniel faithfully relates what God has shown him.

After Daniel relates the meaning of the vision to King Nebuchadnezzar, he implores the king to repent of his arrogance and humble himself before the Lord of Heaven. Although scripture does not specifically tell us the king did not repent, twelve months later—with the assumption that had the king repented, God's judgment would have been averted—judgment is again proclaimed and immediately takes place.

> Twelve months later he was walking on the roof of the royal palace of Babylon. The king reflected and said, 'Is this not Babylon the great, which I myself have built as a royal residence by the might of my power and for the glory of my majesty?' While the word was in the king's mouth, a voice came from heaven, saying, 'King Nebuchadnezzar, to you it is declared: sovereignty has been removed from you, and you will be driven away from mankind, and your dwelling place will be with the beasts of the field. You will be given grass to eat like cattle, and seven periods of time will pass over you until you recognize that the Most High is ruler over the realm of mankind and bestows it on whomever He wishes.' Immediately the word concerning Nebuchadnezzar was fulfilled; and he was driven away from mankind and began eating grass like cattle, and his body was drenched with the dew of heaven until his hair had grown like eagles' feathers and his nails like birds' claws. But at the end of that period, I, Nebuchadnezzar, raised my eyes toward heaven and my reason returned to me, and I blessed the Most High and praised and honored Him who lives forever; For His dominion is an everlasting dominion, And His kingdom endures from generation to generation. All the inhabitants of the earth are accounted as nothing, But He does according to His will in the host of heaven And among the inhabitants of earth; And no one can ward off His hand Or say to Him, 'What have You done?' At that time my reason returned to me. And my majesty and splendor were restored to me for the glory of my kingdom,

and my counselors and my nobles began seeking me out; so I was reestablished in my sovereignty, and surpassing greatness was added to me. Now I, Nebuchadnezzar, praise, exalt and honor the King of heaven, for all His works are true and His ways just, and He is able to humble those who walk in pride. (Daniel 4:29–37)

It is important to take note that there was a period of twelve months between when judgment was originally proclaimed and when it was released into King Nebuchadnezzar's life. We need to take the word of the Lord very seriously and realize that although it may be a long time between what we sow and what we reap—without repentance—His word will always come to pass. In the context of this chapter, we can be sure pride forces God to resist us and that grace flows to the humble.

When the Lord uses circumstances in our lives to bring our pride to the surface, it is essential to our spiritual health that we immediately respond to what He shows us. Our Father will repeatedly bring a character flaw or sin to our attention. If we continue to ignore His admonition, though, He will eventually allow our hearts to harden. It is a scary thought, that because of the hardness of our hearts, we would continue to brush off the God of the universe. The fear of God should grip our hearts, as He never loses track of our responses to His attempts at correction. If we continue to ignore the prompting of the Holy Spirit in our hearts, as a faithful and loving Father, He will have to discipline us—this includes allowing us to reap what we have sown.

It is imperative we learn the lesson of King Nebuchadnezzar. If we respond and repent to the Lord's gentle correction, we can avoid the severity of delayed judgment. If we judge ourselves (agree with what God is showing us), we will not be judged. God's purpose is not to see us suffer loss but to train us into mature children. Even under grace, it is necessary for God to allow trials and tribulation in our lives.

For if we would judge ourselves, we would not be judged. But when we are judged, we are chastened by the Lord, that we may not be condemned with the world. (1 Corinthians 11:31–32, NKJV)

In the case of pride, it is so nauseating to the Lord and has such a potential for destruction to our lives, God must resist us until we humble ourselves under His mighty hand.

You younger men, likewise, be subject to your elders; and all of you, clothe yourselves with humility toward one another, for God is opposed to the proud, but gives grace to the humble. Therefore humble yourselves under the mighty hand of God, that He may exalt you at the proper time. (1 Peter 5:5–6)

The book *The Final Quest* records a vision of major importance to the body of Christ. The author, Rick Joyner, carefully penned—as accurately as he could—the details of the vision. Although I originally read it years ago, the section on the warning of pride has remained with me throughout the years. In a section entitled "The Deadly Trap," the danger of pride—even greater in the higher levels of spiritual growth—is revealed. The vision uses a mountain as the picture of the different levels of spiritual maturity in a Christian's journey to the "top of the mountain." The warriors at the top of the mountain have been through the "Galatians 2:20" level and have reached the level of "the revelation of the Lord's unconditional love."

In the vision, Rick Joyner had reached the top of the mountain, which represents the embodiment of the Lord's unconditional love. As Rick prepared to be sent back down the mountain into battle, the character called Wisdom warned him it was not time yet. Wisdom then instructed him to look in a specific direction. As Rick tried to look in the direction Wisdom was indicating, he was blinded by the glory emanating from his own armor. He finally was able to see a little movement in a small valley below. He then asked Wisdom if there was something he could use to cover the glory of his own armor. Wisdom gave Rick a very plain mantle (cloak) to cover his armor with. Rick asked Wisdom what the cloak represented. Wisdom responded, "Humility. You will not be able to see very well without it."

Rick reluctantly put the cloak of humility on, and he immediately was able to see an entire division of the enemy horde waiting to ambush anyone who came down the mountain. Rick then asked Wisdom what division of the hordes of hell (revealed only when wearing the cloak of humility) it was he could now see. Wisdom's answer is one that should cause us to run from spiritual pride like the plague. He answered, "That is Pride. That is the hardest enemy to see after you have been in the glory. Those who refuse to put on this cloak will suffer much at the hands of that most devious enemy."

As Rick continued to watch the panorama, he saw many of the glorious warriors from the top of the mountain walking blindly into Satan's trap below. As they did, the hordes of hell began to move in from the rear to destroy them. Rick started to run down the mountain to warn the warriors, but Wisdom told him they would not listen to him. Without the cloak of humility, their spiritual pride would blind them to the impending danger and would also harden them toward any warning of the destruction ahead. This lesson has stayed with me through the years and I often ask the Lord to place the "cloak of humility" upon me!

Returning to the illustration of King Nebuchadnezzar in Daniel chapter 5, we see an amazing arrogance in King Nebuchadnezzar's grandson, Belshazzar. This is a startling account of a lesson not learned. In this chapter, Belshazzar is listed as the king's son. However, in the culture of the time, the descendants of a man were all considered his sons and he their father, or as we would say their "forefather." Nonetheless—even as a grandson—King Belshazzar was well-aware of how God had judged his grandfather.

Starting in Daniel 5:1, King Belshazzar is seen holding a huge drinking feast for 1,000 of his nobles. Between the presence of so many underlings and the impressive layout of food and excessive drink, Belshazzar's pride takes over. He soon gives orders for the gold and silver vessels, which were taken by King Nebuchadnezzar from the temple in Jerusalem, to be brought to the feast for all to drink from. At this point Belshazzar went too far. Scripture says they "praised the gods of gold and silver, of bronze, iron, wood and stone" (Daniel 5:4). Immediately after, a hand appeared and wrote God's judgment against Belshazzar on the wall.

The king eventually heard of Daniel's spiritual gifts and called for Daniel to interpret the writing on the wall. Before giving the meaning of the words on the wall, Daniel summarized what God had done to humble King Nebuchadnezzar and how King Belshazzar had ignored God's sovereignty and power.

O king, the Most High God granted sovereignty, grandeur, glory and majesty to Nebuchadnezzar your father. (Daniel 5:18)

But when his heart was lifted up and his spirit became so proud that he behaved arrogantly, he was deposed from his royal throne and his glory was taken away from him. (Daniel 5:20)

Yet you, his son, Belshazzar, have not humbled your heart, even though you knew all this, but you have exalted yourself against the Lord of heaven; and they have brought the vessels of His house before you, and you and your nobles, your wives and your concubines have been drinking wine from them; and you have praised the gods of silver and gold, of bronze, iron, wood and stone, which do not see, hear or understand. But the God in whose hand are your life-breath and all your ways, you have not glorified. (Daniel 5:22–23)

Daniel then proceeded to give the interpretation of the writing on the wall, which proclaimed God's judgment on Belshazzar. The king was slain that very night. It is important to note King Nebuchadnezzar was humbled as a result of God's judgment, and his repentance resulted in a second chance. Whereas, Belshazzar had not been touched by God's significant judgment on his grandfather. Due to the hardness of his heart, Belshazzar's sentence was executed the very night Daniel was used to proclaim God's judgment upon him.

Although this story is an Old-Testament or old-covenant story, the Lord has not changed and still has many ways to humble the proud.

> Whoever exalts himself [with haughtiness and empty pride] shall be humbled [brought low], and whoever humbles himself [whoever has a modest opinion of himself and behaves accordingly] shall be raised to honor. (Matthew 23:12, AMPC)

Humility is a fruit of the Spirit, which can be attained only through the grace of God. We cannot make ourselves humble any more than we can produce any other characteristic of Christ. However, a healthy 'fear' of pride will help us resist even a hint of pride in our hearts—through total dependence on the grace of God.

We have only this life—with the struggles of our flesh, the trials and temptations from the hordes of hell, and the fallen state of man and creation—for the humility of Christ to be imparted to us and through us. When we enter our glorified bodies, our chance to be conformed to the image of Christ, through our love-obedience to Him, will be over. Our opportunity to be an expression of His life in the midst of darkness will have passed away, leaving only "new heavens and a new earth on which righteousness dwells" (2 Peter 3:13b).

Until then, the ultimate prayer of humility we can embrace was penned by the late A.B. Simpson: "God give us the divine insignia of heavenly rank: a bowed head and a meek and lowly spirit."[10]

[10.] *Days of Heaven on Earth*, A.B. Simpson, December 19th

CHAPTER 9

The Beatitudes:
What Kingdom Life Looks Like
Blessed Are They Who Hunger
and Thirst for Righteousness

So Jesus said to the twelve, "You do not want to go away also, do you?" Simon Peter answered Him, "Lord, to whom shall we go? You have words of eternal life."

—John 6:67–68

The setting for the last part of John chapter 6 is that of Jesus teaching a group of disciples (not just the twelve) some of what would shortly be coming to pass. Jesus had made several statements some considered 'hard,' and many had turned away. In the midst of this scene, the apostle Peter speaks from the depth of personal experience with Jesus, "Lord, to whom shall we go? You have words of eternal life."

The revelation of Jesus Christ had been birthed in Peter's heart as he followed the Lord. Peter was not able to go back to life as it was before he met the Savior because Jesus had the "words of eternal life." If by this statement Peter were only referring to the truth of the gospel, he could have embraced Christ as Savior and went home. However, as a result of living with the Lord while He walked the earth, Jesus' presence had become a lifeline to Peter. There was no substitute!

His Manifest Presence

The equivalent of Jesus' presence in our day is the 'manifest presence' of the Holy Spirit. God sent the Holy Spirit to the earth at Pentecost so His abiding presence would remain on earth. The term 'manifest presence' simply means the tangible presence of the Holy Spirit is so intense it is apparent to one of our five senses. He makes Himself manifest to get our attention. He desires to see if we have enough interest in being with Him to turn aside from our normal routine to discover why He has honored us with a special visit.

As we experience the manifest presence of the Holy Spirit we will have a chance to "hunger and thirst" after His presence or to ignore His invitation and go on with life as usual. Honoring His manifest presence is not 'seeking signs' or running after 'emotional experiences.' It is the process of becoming so sensitive to the Holy Spirit that He can manifest Himself in a way that would not be possible without this increased sensitivity.

A Living Sacrifice

Scripture exhorts us to offer our bodies as a living sacrifice. A living sacrifice was an animal brought to the temple as an offering to the Lord. However, rather than being killed, it was left alive to be used in the service of the temple for the rest of its life. The animal's life was not its own and neither is the life of any true child of God.

> Therefore, brothers, I call on you through the compassions of God to present your bodies a living sacrifice, holy, pleasing to God, which is your reasonable service. (Romans 12:1, LITV)

As we become more attune to the moving of the Holy Spirit in our lives, our sensitivity to His prompting increases and we will be able to be used more and more by the Lord. The more we allow the

Lord to use us, the more time—by default—we will be spending in His manifest presence. This will result in a spiral of ever-increasing glory until we cannot live without the tangible awareness of His life on a daily—if not moment-by-moment—basis. This will not leave us 'too heavenly minded to be of any earthly good' but will finally make us fit to walk this earth for the purpose with which we were born—to be like Him!

The Choice Is Yours

Since there are degrees of intimacy with Christ, we will always have a choice as to which spiritual level we choose to live on. The extent we hunger and thirst after righteousness (after Christ, Who is our righteousness) will determine our rate of spiritual growth and our resulting usefulness to our Heavenly Father.

The personal intimacy of those who walked with Christ illustrates different degrees of hungering and thirsting for Him. The bible shows the closest person in His life was John, the Beloved, who laid his head on Jesus' breast. Then, there were Peter, James, and John and after that, the 12 apostles. There was also the 70, who were sent out to minister to the needs of the people and the 120 (plus women) in the upper room waiting for the promise of the Holy Spirit. Lastly, there were multitudes of curious onlookers who flocked around Him but never embraced Him as their Messiah. Each person in these social circles around Christ made a personal choice as to how near they wanted to be to Him. The level of their intimacy with Him was a direct result of the intensity of their desire to be in His presence.

Exceptions to the Norm

There are several accounts in scripture where God, in His sovereignty, shows predetermined favor or disfavor upon individuals. One example of this is when God chose Jacob over Esau while they were still in Rebekah's womb: "Jacob, I loved, but Esau I hated" (Romans 9:13). Since God declared His favor toward Jacob—the younger of the two—before the twins were even born, His decision had nothing to do with their personal response to Him.

Specific examples such as this would make it seem our personal choices are not important. However, in the title text for this chapter, the Lord gave each and every person the opportunity to be "satisfied" to the level of their "hunger and thirst."

> Blessed are those who hunger and thirst for righteousness, for they shall be satisfied. (Matthew 5:6)

The only limitation upon our being completely "satisfied" with all Jesus has and is for us, is the intensity of our passion for Him and all He represents. After all, what else would we hunger for and where else could we go?

Elisha—A Model of Persistence

One of the keys in scripture to being "satisfied" or "filled" (KJV) is persistence. For this reason, we will study several different bible characters to see the role their persistence and faithfulness played in the fulfillment of their God-given destiny. One account of such perseverance is recorded in 2 Kings, chapter 2. Elijah was about to be caught up into heaven, and Elisha was God's choice to receive Elijah's mantle.

> And it came about when the LORD was about to take up Elijah by a whirlwind to heaven, that Elijah went with Elisha from Gilgal. Elijah said to Elisha, "Stay here please, for the LORD has sent me as far as Bethel." But Elisha said, "As the LORD lives and as you yourself live, I will not leave you." So they went down to Bethel. Then the sons of the prophets who were at Bethel came out to Elisha and said to him, "Do you know that the LORD will take away your master from over you today?" And he said, "Yes, I know; be still." Elijah said to him, "Elisha, please stay here, for the LORD has sent me to Jericho." But he said, "As the LORD lives, and as you yourself live, I will not leave you." So they came to Jericho. The sons of the prophets who were at

Jericho approached Elisha and said to him, "Do you know that the LORD will take away your master from over you today?" And he answered, "Yes, I know; be still." Then Elijah said to him, "Please stay here, for the LORD has sent me to the Jordan." And he said, "As the LORD lives, and as you yourself live, I will not leave you." So the two of them went on. Now fifty men of the sons of the prophets went and stood opposite them at a distance, while the two of them stood by the Jordan. Elijah took his mantle and folded it together and struck the waters, and they were divided here and there, so that the two of them crossed over on dry ground. When they had crossed over, Elijah said to Elisha, "Ask what I shall do for you before I am taken from you." And Elisha said, "Please, let a double portion of your spirit be upon me." He said, "You have asked a hard thing. Nevertheless, if you see me when I am taken from you, it shall be so for you; but if not, it shall not be so." As they were going along and talking, behold, there appeared a chariot of fire and horses of fire which separated the two of them. And Elijah went up by a whirlwind to heaven. Elisha saw it and cried out, "My father, my father, the chariots of Israel and its horsemen!" And he saw Elijah no more. Then he took hold of his own clothes and tore them in two pieces. He also took up the mantle of Elijah that fell from him and returned and stood by the bank of the Jordan. He took the mantle of Elijah that fell from him and struck the waters and said, "Where is the LORD, the God of Elijah?" And when he also had struck the waters, they were divided here and there; and Elisha crossed over. (2 Kings 2:1–14)

From the beginning of this account, it is inferred Elijah knew his 'home-going' was imminent. From the inference in verse 2, it would also seem God had let Elisha know that Elijah's departure was near. As a note of interest, it is also clearly stated further down in the text, the sons of the prophets in Bethel and Jericho also had an indication of the nearness of Elijah's departure. In any case, it is not until verse 10 that Elijah clearly reveals to Elisha the condition upon which he would receive the double portion of Elijah's spirit.

The question that still remains is, why did Elijah try to talk Elisha out of being with him when he was taken up to heaven? Although the text does not clearly state why, commentaries frequently suggest three explanations for this portion of scripture. The first thought is Elijah may have had an indication of the magnificent glory and power God would display when he was taken up to heaven. Knowing this, he may have thought his departure should be a private moment—thinking the moment should not be shared, out of sheer modesty. The second idea is Elijah may have wanted to spare Elisha from being an eyewitness to the event to lessen the grief from the loss of his spiritual father. The last, widely held possibility is that Elijah was testing Elisha to see how determined Elisha was to receive a double portion of his spirit.

Regardless of why God impressed Elijah to handle the situation the way he did, one thing is very clear: There is a good chance Elisha would have forfeited his entire earthly spiritual inheritance—or purpose in life—had he not been persistent. We do know from scripture and from God's dealings with His saints throughout history, that we will always be tested to see if we really want what we say we want.

Proof of Our Faith

One of God's basic principles is that if we are faithful in little, He will give us more. He must test our hearts with the little to see if we will be able to handle the pressure and responsibility of the greater. The fire of testing must be increased until we become living "proof" that what we say we have is real.

> So that the proof of your faith, being more precious than gold which is perishable, even though tested by fire, may be found to result in praise and glory and honor at the revelation of Jesus Christ. (1 Peter 1:7)

By definition, "proof" is only "proof" if those around us can see it. As the Lord brings us through the "refiner's fire" (Malachi 3:2), the evidence that what we say is true will be the coming forth of Christlike strength and character. Our choosing to remain in the fire will result in radical change in our innermost being, including freedom from past bondages. These character improvements surface during times of intense heat and become apparent to us, as well as those around us.

The Rest of the Story

Elisha passed the test of persistence by remaining steadfast to the known will of God. Since it is obvious—although not stated—that he knew Elijah would soon be leaving his presence, he did not let Elijah out of his sight. This was Elisha's determination, even before Elijah informed him of the condition under which he would receive a double portion of his spirit. For that reason, whether due to an understanding of the mantle of Elijah he desired or because of his affection toward the elder prophet, his persistence was rewarded. God was "a rewarder of them that diligently seek him" (Hebrews 11:6, KJV) in Elisha's time and will always be!

Since Elisha overcame every time Elijah attempted to talk him into leaving his presence, Elisha received a double portion of the spirit of God that had been upon Elijah. The only thing Elisha allowed to separate him from Elijah was the chariot of fire and the horses of the Lord! Elisha is a powerful example of a person persistently acting upon what God has revealed—even when Elisha may not have understood all God intended.

We May Not Know It All!

As God arranges the tests in our lives, it will be very common to only have partial knowledge of His immediate plan.

> For we know in part and we prophesy in part; but when the perfect comes, the partial will be done away. (1 Corinthians 13:9–10)

It is necessary for our spiritual growth to be obedient to the known will of God without knowing the 'big picture.' For that matter, our finite minds cannot possibly understand all God is arranging behind the scene on our behalf. If we knew all God was doing, how He was planning to bring it to pass, and His timing, we wouldn't need much faith. Moreover, if His "expected end" always came to pass quickly and literally (as opposed to in types, shadows, wordplay, puns, and painfully long times of waiting), we would never mature to 'faith in His faithfulness' but would be spoiled children. If we knew all the facts and what He was doing in each test, childlike trust in His faithfulness—in the face of the unknown—would never be developed. God will test our love and persistence for righteousness, which is doing things His way—even without an understanding of His "expected end."

> For I know the thoughts that I think toward you, saith the LORD, thoughts of peace, and not of evil, to give you an expected end. (Jeremiah 29:11, KJV)

In the words of Jack Taylor, "God gives information on a need-to-know basis." Even when He has revealed His "expected end" to us, part of each test will be to rest in the promise of His "end" without total knowledge of how and when He plans to get us there. Even as we increase in our ability to hear the Lord and understand His ways in a greater dimension, we must still "know in part" and "prophesy in part." This partial knowledge will continue to strengthen our faith, show our faithfulness to our Father, and protect us from pride and its resulting self-destruction until Jesus returns as the head of His bride.

Ruth—a Picture of Faithfulness

Another classic example showing God as a rewarder of those who diligently seek Him is the account of Ruth the Moabitess. The setting of the book, which bears her name, is the story of a Jewish family sojourning in the land of Moab due to a famine in Bethlehem. The father of the family (Elimelech) died in Moab and the couple's two sons married women from the foreign land. This presented a problem since the Moabites were idol worshippers and did not know the true and living God. After an extended period of time, the two sons died. This left their mother, Naomi, and their two wives, Orpah and Ruth, to fend for themselves. This brings us to Ruth 1:8.

And Naomi said to her two daughters-in-law, "Go, return each of you to her mother's house. May the LORD deal kindly with you as you have dealt with the dead and with me. May the LORD grant that you may find rest, each in the house of her husband." Then she kissed them, and they lifted up their voices and wept. And they said to her, "No, but we will surely return with you to your people." But Naomi said, "Return, my daughters. Why should you go with me? Have I yet sons in my womb, that they may be your husbands? Return, my daughters! Go, for I am too old to have a husband. If I said I have hope, if I should even have a husband tonight and also bear sons, would you therefore wait until they were grown? Would you therefore refrain from marrying? No, my daughters; for it is harder for me than for you, for the hand of the LORD has gone forth against me." And they lifted up their voices and wept again; and Orpah kissed her mother-in-law, but Ruth clung to her. Then she said, "Behold, your sister-in-law has gone back to her people and her gods; return after your sister-in-law." But Ruth said, "Do not urge me to leave you or turn back from following you; for where you go, I will go, and where you lodge, I will lodge. Your people shall be my people, and your God, my God. Where you die, I will die, and there I will be buried. Thus may the LORD do to me, and worse, if anything but death parts you and me." When she saw that she was determined to go with her, she said no more to her. (Ruth 1:8–18)

From Ruth 1:4, we know Ruth had been in Naomi's family for approximately ten years before Naomi made the decision to return to her homeland. The text does not state that Ruth embraced the God of Israel during Naomi's sojourn in Moab, but we do know from Ruth 1:16 that by the time of Naomi's departure from Moab, Ruth had committed herself to the God of Israel: "Your people shall be my people, and your God, my God."

This commitment to Naomi and the God of Israel required Ruth to leave her homeland, her friends, and her family. This was a remarkable decision considering Ruth was a young widow without children and had no one to support her. She really was forsaking all to follow Naomi and her God. If Ruth had counted the cost, the known facts would have cried out to leave Naomi as Orpah had and start over in the land of Moab. As the story continues, we see that the wonderful "expected end" God had for Ruth would never have come to pass had she made the 'sensible' choice, which—according to known facts—she had every right to do.

This account of the Lord's reward for one who followed Him against all odds and against all apparent evidence was preserved in scripture as an eternal testimony of God's faithfulness to those who hunger and thirst for righteousness.

Almost always, the foremost events in our lives will be God's reward for walking by faith—according to the present word of the Lord—when the fulfillment of the word seems impossible. In order to overcome in this life, we must renew our minds to the truth that everything we see with our eyes and all we would consider success on this earth is only temporary. Whereas, all that really matters—since we are eternal beings—is that which is important to God.

> While we look not at the things which are seen, but at the things which are not seen; for the things which are seen are temporal, but the things which are not seen are eternal. (2 Corinthians 4:18)

If this way of life sounds boring to you—a lifestyle to limit your freedom—the exact opposite is true. When we begin to really understand our Heavenly Father's love for us, we will realize He only guides us through the trials and tests of life needed to set us free from 'our self.' Choosing our own way is not freedom, since it leaves us under bondage to sin and 'self.' We are not free until we come into identification with Christ.

Ruth's decision to deny herself and follow the true God set her free to receive the abundant life He had for her and has for every one of us. A very important detail in this account is that Ruth could not have had any idea of what God had in store for her when she left Moab. She followed her mother-in-law by the leading of her heart and by faith in Naomi's God. The same will hold true for us. Our continual challenge will be to follow the path God sets before us— one moment, one hour, one day at a time—without insisting on understanding what the Lord is doing each step of the way.

Due to her faithfulness, Ruth's story ends with the Lord giving her more than she could have ever imagined.

> Now to Him who, in exercise of His power that is at work within us, is able to do infinitely beyond all our highest prayers or thoughts. (Ephesians 3:20, 1912 Weymouth NT)

The Reward of Faithfulness

The Lord led Ruth to glean grain on the land of a kinsman of her deceased father-in-law, Elimelech. According to Jewish law, the nearest kinsman could choose to take his relative's widow as his wife so she would be provided for and be able to have children as a godly heritage. The Lord led Ruth to the fields of Boaz, who chose to exercise his right to "redeem" her. Boaz was loving, wealthy, and faithful and was a fairy-tale ending to the harsh beginnings of Ruth's life.

In addition to the Lord's glorious provision for Ruth in her lifetime, He also placed her in the lineage of Christ. She became the great-great...grandmother of the Messiah, as well as an example of a gentile being grafted into the true "olive tree," Who is Christ (Romans 11:24).

Ruth's hunger and thirst for righteousness not only resulted in great blessing for her, but Naomi's life was also redeemed through Ruth's faithfulness. Had Ruth chosen according to 'common sense' or according to the way she had the 'right' to choose, she would have lost the magnificent end God had for her and for Naomi. Since she let God choose her path, she was greatly blessed. We, too, will never regret choosing God's way for us if we are faithful to the end. Often, it is only at His "expected end" that we see God's great faithfulness and love in what He has allowed in our lives.

We used the word 'faithfulness' to describe the attribute which led Ruth to the position that allowed the Lord to bestow upon her all He desired. Our Heavenly Father receives great delight in pouring out His favor upon His children who have been tested and have come forth as gold. The problem is, few will pay the price necessary to have the intimacy with the Lord that is required to keep them in the center of His will. Being in the center of His will is not to say we are without sin, but that as the Holy Spirit corrects, we respond with repentance. Whether we stray from the path in attitude, word, or deed, our response should be one of "godly sorrow" (2 Corinthians 7:10, KJV), restitution when necessary, and change of direction. This attitude of being concerned with what God cares about—above all else—will keep us on the path of faithfulness.

Daniel—Faithful No Matter What

Our final example of hungering and thirsting for righteousness concerns the faithfulness of one of God's choice servants. Daniel's life is a portrait of 'faithfulness,' which I define as "adhering to the known will of God without exception." If the thought of this seems impossible to you, once our will is broken, there is a place—in union with the Lord—where we will no longer desire to do anything contrary to His revealed will for our lives. As we have previously seen, the Lord gives us a new heart (Ezekiel 11:19), He gives us all we need for life and godliness (2 Peter 1:3), and He gives us both the desire and power to do His will (Philippians 2:13). God will never ask anything of us that we cannot accomplish in Him. We can do all things through Christ, Who is our strength (Philippians 4:13).

It is important to remember, God loves us more than we will ever be able to comprehend, and nothing escapes His notice. He longs for mature sons and daughters who will rule and reign with Him for eternity. The pain we endure along the path of the 'crucified life' has enduring purpose. He is very careful in what He allows in our lives, how long He makes us wait, and where He positions us.

Faithfulness requires our unwavering obedience to His faithfulness—even when our finite minds cannot understand His infinite purpose. We must try to wrap our minds around the truth that we are in the hands of the all-powerful God of the universe, Who, at the same time, cares so much about us He stores our tears in a bottle (Psalm 56:8) and knows the number of the hairs on our head (Matthew 10:30). This One, you can trust.

The Life of Daniel

In Daniel 1:2, we are told God gave the king of Judah (the king of God's people) into the hands of the king of Babylon, Nebuchadnezzar. Babylon in scripture is always a picture of the world and all that is against God in any given society. After many years and after repeated warnings through a number of His prophets, the Lord used the ungodly for the judgment of His rebellious people.

In the first chapter of the book of Daniel, the narrative tells of Daniel and three other outstanding youth from the "sons of Israel" (Daniel 1:3). They were chosen to be indoctrinated in the ways of the Chaldeans for eventual service in the king's court. This placed the four young men, who had been raised to honor the only true God, in the complete care and education of a completely heathen king. It is in the midst of this setting that Daniel—an Old-Testament overcomer—pens a prophecy that describes the Day of the Lord's Appearing.

> Those who have insight will shine brightly like the brightness of the expanse of heaven, and those who lead the many to righteousness, like the stars forever and ever. (Daniel 12:3)

By necessity, we must be in darkness in order to shine brightly for the Lord—the greater the darkness, the greater the opportunity to shine. The Lord leads us into darkness to give us the chance to learn to rest in the face of the unknown. He leaves us in the dark long enough to test us—to see if we will choose to remain in discomfort out of love and obedience to Him.

In order to persevere in these unexpected seasons, we must train ourselves to look for God in the everyday things of life—these awkward, unpleasant places are exactly where God has ordained us to be! It is here we will choose, like Daniel, to overcome and shine in the darkness or "fall short of the glory of God" (Romans 3:23).

The first stand Daniel made for the Lord while in captivity was to refuse to "defile himself" with the food or drink provided for the chosen youth.

> But Daniel made up his mind that he would not defile himself with the king's choice food or with the wine which he drank; so he sought permission from the commander of the officials that he might not defile himself. (Daniel 1:8)

The words "made up his mind" imply a 'determined resolution' or a 'heart commitment.' Similar to Elisha, we are not told specifically why Daniel knew the king's food and drink would defile him, but the commentaries give several insights. The food may have been that which was forbidden by the Law of Moses and would have defiled him in a ceremonial sense. It was also common at the time for the king's food and wine to first be offered to Bel and then blessed in the pagan god's name. This probability would certainly have been against Daniel's conscience. The whole principle of partaking of the "king's choice food" and "wine" would have given Daniel's sanction to a lifestyle inconsistent with his principles (wine, in itself, was not the issue—see Daniel 10:3). Like Moses, Daniel chose "to suffer affliction with the people of God, than to enjoy the pleasures of sin for a season" (Hebrews 11:25, KJV).

Daniel 1:15 documents that at the end of ten days of testing by their Babylonian overseer, the youth were "fatter" and their countenance "better" than the youth who had been eating from the king's table. Daniel's devotion in his pursuit of righteousness affected the health and physical appearance of the four youth. His determined resolution, as we can see from verse 17, was also greatly honored by the Lord.

As for these four youths, God gave them knowledge and intelligence in every branch of literature and wisdom; Daniel even
understood all kinds of visions and dreams. (Daniel 1:17)

Due to Daniel's faithfulness, he received the gift of understanding "all kinds of visions and dreams." As we continue with the narrative of Daniel's life, the progressive importance of continued adher-
ence to the known will of God unfolds. The gift of interpretation of
visions and dreams Daniel received from his initial faithfulness to the
Lord was the foundation for the next step in God's plan.

After the time of testing (in regard to food and drink), Daniel,
his three friends, and the rest of youth who had been readied for
the king's service, were presented to King Nebuchadnezzar. The
four Jewish youth were found to be ten times wiser and with more
understanding than the others and were placed in the king's personal
service.

The Revealing of God's Plan

In the second year of Nebuchadnezzar's reign, he had a series
of dreams that were greatly disturbing to him. The king called all of
his magicians, conjurers, sorcerers, and master astrologers together
to tell him what his dreams were and to interpret them. The group
tried desperately to get the king to tell them the dream so they could
at least make up an interpretation, but he was wise to their schemes.
Instead, the king commanded all the wise men in Babylon to be
destroyed because of their failure to reveal his dream.

When the captain of the king's bodyguard came to kill Daniel
and his friends, Daniel asked for time to seek the Lord for the answer
to the mysteries the king had been shown in his dreams. Due to
Daniel's singular love and devotion to the Lord, God delighted in
giving him the dream and its interpretation.

Because he has loved Me, therefore I will deliver him; I will set
him securely on high, because he has known My name. He will

call upon Me, and I will answer him; I will be with him in trouble; I will rescue him and honor him. (Psalm 91:14–15)

When commenting on this passage, A.B. Simpson, the founder of the Christian and Missionary Alliance, said, "God takes a peculiar pride in revealing His love to the heart that wholly chooses Him. Heaven and earth will fade away before its trust can be disappointed."

Daniel and his friends certainly were not disappointed. Due to the fact that God gave Daniel the dream and interpretation, the lives of all the wise men in Babylon were spared. God was magnified in a heathen land, and Daniel and his friends were set up as rulers over the kingdom—"Blessed are those who hunger and thirst for righteousness." The four youth certainly were blessed!

In light of Daniel's life so far, we can see the definitions of "blessed" from earlier chapters describe his life. It could have been said Daniel was "happy—to be envied," "spiritually prosperous," and "fortunate." It is also true he had "a happiness from the revelation of God's matchless grace" and a "joy and satisfaction in God's favor and salvation regardless of his outward conditions." All of these statements are descriptions of the "blessed" man!

The rest of the book of Daniel shows how God continued to protect him throughout his life. His favor even continued through the reign of several kings. In fact, in Daniel 9:23 and again in Daniel 10:11, an angel from God refers to Daniel as a man that is "highly esteemed." The words used for highly esteemed literally mean "desirable" or "precious." What amazing terms of love and intimacy God used to describe His faithful servant! Nothing on earth or in heaven is worth more than the knowledge of our Father's favor and generosity toward those who "hunger and thirst for righteousness."

Seeking God for Who He Is

Inherent to hungering and thirsting for righteousness is seeking God for Who He is and not for what He gives. When we first come to know the Lord, there is a natural drawing to the God Who hears every cry of our heart. In spiritual infancy, the Lord shows Himself as the God Who provides our every need and delights in blessing His children. God's character never changes, but as we mature, the Lord must deal with us differently for training in righteousness. The personal fine-tuning of our training is designed to lead us into an intimate relationship with our Heavenly Bridegroom.

As intimacy with the Lord—whether Father, Son, or Holy Spirit—is perfected, we come to a point where we are 'addicted' to His presence. This is not a weakness or a negative dependence but a return to the original relationship God had with Adam in the garden. The discipline of the Lord in our lives is designed to bring such a trust and a reality of His love for us, that our love in return is strengthened. Eventually, our love for Him is so deep we would not want to live a day without the tangible presence of His love.

There are many examples in scripture of people who came to the place of wanting intimacy with the Lord—regardless of what He did or did not give them. For that matter, throughout the bible there is an awesome reverence for God and a respect for His power. The men who penned scripture were amazed God had anything to do with man, let alone that He would desire to be a friend with the creatures He created.

> What is man that You take thought of him, And the son of man that You care for him? (Psalm 8:4)

In fact, one hindrance to intimacy with God in biblical times was an unhealthy fear of God—they feared getting close to Him. In our day, the hindrance to such a relationship with the Almighty is that we are so self-sufficient we have no need to 'bother' with His interference in our lives or with His insistence on changing us into His image.

It has been said the modern-day church is idolatrous—not because we worship objects made with our own hands but because we have fashioned a "god" after the imagination of our hearts. We have formed in our minds an image of what we think God is like or how we would like Him to be. Then, in idolatry, we have chosen to only embrace the "god" of our own design.

If our minds think like 21st century America, we are destined to defeat. We are transformed by the renewing of our minds (Romans 12:2). Because of this, we will not experience the Kingdom of Heaven without a radical change of mind. For this reason, I feel we need to take the time to study the attitudes of several overcomers in the Old Testament.

Job—No Strings Attached

One classic example of a man who worshipped God for Who He is, as opposed to what He could give, is Job. In the first chapter of the book of Job, we find the narrative of Satan presenting himself before the Lord—possibly for the purpose of accusing the brethren. When the Lord asked Satan if he had considered the uprightness of Job, his reply was cynical. Satan continued with the accusation that Job only feared God because he understood the abundance in his life was a result of God's protection. This accusation led to God giving Satan permission to afflict all Job had—apart from touching Job, himself.

The story of Job is very familiar to many of us, but what we want to look at is Job's attitude after all God allowed Satan to inflict upon Him. These statements show Job hungered and thirsted after righteousness—for God alone—and not for what God had given him. After the first attack from Satan in chapter 1 of Job, we read of Job's remarkable reaction and reply.

> Then Job arose and tore his robe and shaved his head, and he fell to the ground and worshiped. He said, "Naked I came from my mother's womb, And naked I shall return there. The LORD gave and the LORD has taken away. Blessed be the name of the LORD." Through all this Job did not sin nor did he blame God. (Job 1:20–22)

There are scriptures that refer to God's prosperity, His many blessings, and His giving us the desires of our heart. Nevertheless, the timing and choosing of what He gives must be left to Him. He is the only One Who sees the universal 'big picture' and the only One Who knows exactly what is in our best interest. We must trust in His love for us over our own understanding.

This trust, as well as Job's godly character, is again revealed in his answer to his wife in chapter 2 of Job.

> But he said to her, "You speak as one of the foolish women speaks. Shall we indeed accept good from God and not accept adversity?" In all this Job did not sin with his lips. (Job 2:10)

To seek God chiefly because we expect to have a better life is not hungering and thirsting for Him but is self-centered. Typically, a life sold out for God will be visibly blessed, but seeking to be blessed is not a righteous motivation. There are many stories of Christians whose lives were completely dedicated to God and were very fruitful in the spirit but were not 'materially successful.'

The Lord has a plan and a destiny for each of us as He conforms us to His image. Our part is to not have an agenda of our own but to only love Him and walk in obedience to His revealed will. We need to guard our hearts so that our focus is on our daily fellowship with the Lord and not on what we expect from Him. When we delight in the Lord, He gives us the desires of our heart (Psalm 37:4). When we do, we will delight in what He gives us because the choice was left to Him.

The final statement from Job that reveals his heart for God is found in chapter 13:

> Though He slay me, yet will I trust in Him. (Job 13:15a, KJV)

Since the time of Christ, Christians have lost their lives for just claiming to be one of His followers. Many of our brothers and sisters throughout church history have also suffered much persecution for refusing to be silenced as they proclaimed the truths of scripture. Even today, in the 21st century, persecution and martyrdom are commonplace in much of the world. First and foremost, we must seek God for Who He is, be ready to "consider it all joy" (James 1:2) to suffer for Christ, and be prepared to die for Him. The life of a man, who is not ready to die for His God, will be of little worth in His kingdom.

Moses—Friend of God

Another picture of desiring to know the Lord as a friend and not just as a benefactor is the account of Moses leading God's people in their wilderness journey. Moses desired to know God in a personal way, which was totally unprecedented at that time in history. Moses was a Jew and, as such, was a member of the race God had chosen to be His people. Through God's direct intervention, Moses was raised in a heathen pharaoh's palace, only to flee for his life to the wilderness, where he tended flocks for 40 years. Yet, through all of this, deep within his heart was a desire to know an infinite God. If we thought in the natural, the idea of desiring a close relationship with the God of the universe—after murdering a man and running into the wilderness—would seem presumptuous on the part of Moses. Nevertheless, this is exactly what the heart of God desires. In Exodus 33, Moses' desire toward the Lord is expressed.

> "Now therefore, I pray You, if I have found favor in Your sight, let me know Your ways that I may know You, so that I may find favor in Your sight. Consider too, that this nation is Your people." And He said, "My presence shall go with you, and I will give you rest." Then he said to Him, "If Your presence does not go with us, do not lead us up from here. For how then can it be known that I have found favor in Your sight, I and Your people? Is it not by Your going with us, so that we, I and Your people, may be distinguished from all the other people who are upon the face of the earth?" (Exodus 33:13–16)

Moses—just a man—stood before God and said, "If I have found favor in Your sight, let me know Your ways." God was so pleased by Moses' desire, He assured Moses His presence would be with him and that He would give Moses "rest." [11] These two graces from the Lord are still the signs of those who know their God.

The next scene that shows Moses' special relationship with God is from Exodus 20. Moses and the people of Israel were camped at the base of Mount Sinai, and the glory of the Lord was upon the mountain. In this visitation, the Lord's glory appeared as fire and smoke, thunder and lightning flashes, the sound of a trumpet, and as the mountain quaking. Since the people did not understand God's ways, His unique presence caused them to fear and drawback from God.

> The people trembled with fear when they heard the thunder and the trumpet and saw the lightning and the smoke coming from the mountain. They stood a long way off and said to Moses, "If you speak to us, we will listen. But don't let God speak to us, or we will die!" "Don't be afraid!" Moses replied. "God has come only to test you, so that by obeying him you won't sin." But when Moses went near the thick cloud where God was, the people stayed a long way off. (Exodus 20:18–21, CEV)

If the people had been gripped with the fear of God, the draw toward Him would have been greater than their fear of the manifestation of His glory. However, without an understanding of His ways, their fear controlled them and they drew back from His presence. God purposely 'tested' them to see if their desire to know Him would propel them beyond their comfort zone, but they failed the test. On the other hand, Moses' desire to know God gave him the grace to approach "the thick cloud where God was."

God Has Not Changed

God has not changed. Still today, He purposely comes in ways we are not expecting in order to test us. Even as He arranged for Jesus to be born in humble circumstances to challenge the religious think-

---

[11.] See the "Sabbath rest" (Hebrews 3, 4)

ers of the day, He continues to move in ways that challenge what we think we know of Him.

It is important to remember the two graces God gave Moses because of his desire to know His ways: His presence and His rest. In order to overcome and be a part of the 'special forces' of the Lord's last day army, we will have to walk in His manifest presence. It is in His presence that we are restored, changed into His image, and where an understanding of His ways is 'downloaded' into our spirits. It is in the total surrender of the right to our lives and by identifying with the death, burial, and resurrection of Jesus that we enter His rest. These two spiritual exercises are necessary to know God. Without them, our self-life remains intact, and God will not entrust the secrets of His heart to "flesh."

The children of Israel knew "His acts" because of His miraculous provision for them in their exodus from Egypt and from their years in the wilderness. Nevertheless, they still chose to stay "a long way off" from His presence at Mount Sinai. In contrast to the Israelites, Moses pushed through to the presence of the Lord and insisted on knowing His ways. At the Lord's return, will you be found in the company of Moses or with the sons of Israel?

He made known His ways to Moses, His acts to the sons of Israel. (Psalm 103:7)

The Maturing of the Bride

Our last example of seeking God for Who He is may be found in the book of the Song of Solomon. The Song of Solomon teaches us the progression of spiritual maturity in the life of a believer—from new birth to ruling and reigning with our Lord.

In the beginning of our spiritual walk, we are enthralled with all the Lord does for us—and rightfully so. Typically, we then move into a season of feverish activity, working for Him. A response to His goodness and a desire to be around what is happening in His church compel us into action. After a period of time, with an unrealistic pace of Christian service, there is the danger of suffering burnout from extreme activity done in the power of our flesh. There is also an increasing disillusionment with the humanity of Christ's body. It is here the Lord tries to get our attention and challenge us to balance working for Him with becoming like Him. At this point, rather than responding to God's invitation to come and know Him in an intimate way, many turn away from the things of God.

The Bride in the Song of Solomon finds herself exhausted but is still drawn to her beloved. She doesn't understand total commitment or the deeper things of God, but she is attracted to the thought of an intimate relationship with Him. In the end of the second chapter of the Song of Solomon, she expresses the level of surrender she is at.

> My beloved is mine, and I am his. (Song of Solomon 2:16a)

At this point in her spiritual growth, the bride is responding to the wooing of her beloved and is in love with Him because He has been so good to her—and so He has. Her heart is revealed in her emphasis on her beloved being hers and in her reply that she is His. This is not wrong on her behalf. This is not, however, where the Lord intends for her to remain. As their relationship matures, she is found to proclaim that she is her beloved's no matter what her circumstances.

> I am my beloved's, And his desire is for me. (Song of Solomon 7:10)

Her expression of being her beloved's is a complete surrender to the rights to her life. Her knowledge that His desire is for her is confirmation of His favor in response to her unconditional love.

> I love those who love me; And those who diligently seek me will find me. (Proverbs 8:17)

At long last, the bride is found "leaning on her beloved" as she emerges from the wilderness, which was a prolonged season of testing in her life. She has responded positively to the Lord's dealings with her and has come to the place where she knows without Him she can do nothing.

> Who is this coming up from the wilderness Leaning on her beloved? (Song of Solomon 8:5)

> I am the vine, you are the branches; he who abides in Me and I in him, he bears much fruit, for apart from Me you can do nothing. (John 15:5)

From the place of unconditional surrender and total dependence on the Lord, the bride is ready to be trained for ruling and reigning with her beloved. She went from seeking the Lord in response to what He had given her, to an unfeigned love for Him, no matter what the cost. This is the progression of spiritual maturity in the life of a believer.

The key to an upward progression in our spiritual growth is to "hunger and thirst for righteousness." When we seek the Lord for Who He is, apart from what He gives us, we have His guarantee that we "shall be satisfied."

The Lord is looking for a people who have been so transformed by His power that they become an expression of Him on this earth. His ultimate plan is for a 'many-membered body' to walk this earth as He did. This body will be made up of common people whose "hunger and thirst for righteousness" have qualified them to be a part of the Lord's last day army, through which His glory will be revealed.

CHAPTER 10

The Beatitudes:
What Kingdom Life Looks Like
Blessed Are the Merciful

Blessed are the merciful, for they shall receive mercy.
—Matthew 5:7

As I have studied the Beatitudes, it has become very clear our cooperation with God is vital for His kingdom to be expressed on the earth. Although His will shall be done and His kingdom will come to earth, as it is in heaven, we can personally suffer loss as to the part we will play in the purposes of God. Qualifying to become a vessel of God's mercy on earth is no exception to the pattern we see developing. We will only be a "vessel" of mercy "useful to the Master" (2 Timothy 2:21), to the degree we allow the Lord to change us into His image.

What We Sow, We Will Also Reap

This Beatitude expresses the biblical law of sowing and reaping. As the Creator of the universe, God's laws are in effect whether He is acknowledged or not—what we sow, we will also reap.

> Do not be deceived, God is not mocked; for whatever a man sows, this he will also reap. For the one who sows to his own flesh will from the flesh reap corruption, but the one who sows to the Spirit will from the Spirit reap eternal life. (Galatians 6:7–8)

The word translated as "corruption" has the meaning, "decay" or "ruin."[12] When we operate in the flesh, we will reap a decline in the quality of life. The more we allow the flesh to rule in our lives, the greater the decline will be. We could feasibly allow this decline to continue to the point of ruin. Since mercy is a facet of God's character, it comes forth by yielding to and depending on the Holy Spirit. Conversely, if we choose to be merciless, we are sowing to the flesh and from the flesh we will always reap "corruption."

Even unbelievers observe the reality of the principle of sowing and reaping. With little or no biblical knowledge, it is apparent from life's experiences that what we sow is what we reap. In the world, the law of sowing and reaping sounds like, "What goes around, comes around." Even outside the church, this 'golden rule' was taught for years as a warning!

> Treat others the same way you want them to treat you. (Luke 6:31)

The mercy you extend to others in your daily walk will have a marked effect on how merciful your Heavenly Father can be to you. In fact, there is scriptural evidence that not only do we reap what we sow, but proportionately, we reap more than we sow—whether good or bad!

> For they sow the wind and they reap the whirlwind. (Hosea 8:7a)

[12.] Amplified Bible, e-sword

Be merciful, just as your Father is merciful. Do not judge, and you will not be judged; and do not condemn, and you will not be condemned; pardon, and you will be pardoned. Give, and it will be given to you. They will pour into your lap a good measure—pressed down, shaken together, and running over. For by your standard of measure it will be measured to you in return. (Luke 6:36–38)

If you pronounce judgment, you will receive judgment—"pressed down, shaken together, and running over." If you release condemnation, you will receive condemnation—"pressed down, shaken together, and running over." On the other hand, if you issue a pardon (or in other words, if you release an offender from any responsibility for the offense), you will be pardoned—"pressed down, shaken together, and running over." By your standard of measure, if you are merciful, you will receive mercy!

Forcing God's Hand

So speak and so act as those who are to be judged by the law of liberty. For judgment will be merciless to one who has shown no mercy; mercy triumphs over judgment. (James 2:12–13)

Besides reaping what we sow, our lack of mercy actually forces God's hand of judgment against us. When teaching on forgiveness in Matthew 18, Jesus shared a very solemn parable to illustrate the result of not showing mercy. The parable starts in verse 23, with the Kingdom of Heaven being compared to the story of a king who was settling accounts with his slaves. The first slave in line owed the king 10,000 talents (one talent being worth more than fifteen years' wages for a common laborer). In other words, there was absolutely no way the slave could have ever repaid the king. Since the slave could not possibly pay what he owed, the king ordered him, his wife and children, and all that he owned to be sold as payment for the debt. The slave fell to the ground, asking the king to be patient until he could pay the debt. The king's merciful reply is recorded in verse 27.

> And the lord of that slave felt compassion and released him and forgave him the debt. (Matthew 18:27)

The king's response contains two keywords for us to remember: compassion and release. Many times in our self-righteousness, we think much more highly of ourselves than we ought and fail to release compassion. In a state of blindness to our own faults, we can fail to realize that we, too, are in need of mercy.

We can justify of our lack of compassion in many ways. We are prone to think we would never end up in 'that' situation—relying on our abilities and hard work rather than on the mercy of God. In our deception and hidden pride, we become living examples of Christ's teaching in Matthew 7:1–3.

> Do not judge so that you will not be judged. For in the way you judge, you will be judged; and by your standard of measure, it will be measured to you. Why do you look at the speck that is in your brother's eye, but do not notice the log that is in your own eye? (Matthew 7:1–3)

The king had compassion and pardoned the slave. If we fail to have compassion on those around us—even if it's just the driver who cuts us off in traffic, the extremely slow store clerk, or the neighbor who continually seems to mismanage his life—we force our King to treat us in the same way. Our attitudes and actions force God's hand of judgment against us.

Since this is such a serious matter, we need to ask the Holy Spirit to convict us when we are critical and intolerant—even like an alarm—warning us of what may come if we fail to repent. The first two verses of Romans chapter 2 are another sobering witness to the destruction we may reap if we ignore the warnings in God's word.

> Therefore you have no excuse, everyone of you who passes judgment, for in that which you judge another, you condemn yourself; for you who judge practice the same things. And we know

that the judgment of God rightly falls upon those who practice such things. (Romans 2:1–2)

According to these verses, not only can our attitudes force the hand of God's judgment upon us, but it "rightly falls upon" us. In other words, we deserve it!

Therefore there is now no condemnation for those who are in Christ Jesus. For the law of the Spirit of life in Christ Jesus has set you free from the law of sin and of death. (Romans 8:1–2)

Although we are not under condemnation in Christ, we can experientially remove ourselves out from under "the law of the Spirit of life in Christ Jesus" and force God to judge us as if we were still under "the law of sin and of death." If we choose to be unmerciful and condemning, rather than being "judged by the law of liberty" (James 2:12), we force God to judge us in the same manner we have judged.

It is vital for the body of Christ to understand this principle! In the meantime, we are suffering great loss—both corporately and personally—due to our lack of compassion and mercy. This is tragic, since the bible clearly teaches how to avoid God's judgment by walking in mercy and grace.

This brings us back to Matthew 18:27. The king in this parable not only had compassion on the slave but then "released" the slave from any responsibility from his indebtedness. In respect to our Heavenly King, what He did for us is far better. Not only are we released from any responsibility for our failing, but positionally, we are also "justified" (Romans 5:9)—just as if we had never sinned. Even the remembrance of our sin is erased!

The parable of the king and his slave goes on to tell us the forgiven slave also had someone indebted to him. Even after having been forgiven more than he could ever repay, the slave went after the one who owed him—demanding payment. The slave not only searched out his debtor but grabbed him—choking him as he insisted on payment of the sum owed. As the man fell to the ground, he pleaded for forgiveness from the forgiven slave. With no compassion or mercy, the one who had been forgiven such a great debt threw the man into prison, rather than releasing him from a debt equal to only a day's wages. Upon seeing the forgiven slave's behavior toward his debtor, his fellow slaves went to the king and told him what they had seen.

> Then summoning him, his lord said to him, "You wicked slave, I forgave you all that debt because you pleaded with me. Should you not also have had mercy on your fellow slave, in the same way that I had mercy on you?" And his lord, moved with anger, handed him over to the torturers until he should repay all that was owed him. (Matthew 18:32–34)

As to what the "torturers" refer to, there are varying opinions. One very likely school of thought is that over 80 percent of all illness is psychosomatic. This does not mean the symptoms are imaginary but that they are caused from turmoil in our soul, which is the seat of our mind, will, and emotions. If we refuse to forgive, extend mercy, and walk in grace, the negative effects on our mind, will, and emotions can cause many—even significant—diseases in our souls, as well as our bodies. Another explanation of the torturers is demonic spirits being loosed into our lives because of our lack of mercy. These spirits could include spirits of hatred, anger, anxiety, addiction or any number of conditions that will rob us of our quality of life.

Although we may not know exactly what was released into the life of the unforgiving slave, we do know one thing: he was handed "over to the torturers." This word picture alone should give us a healthy fear of walking contrary to the mercy of God.

As we see from scripture, it is clearly God's will for us to be merciful in every situation. It is important, however, to keep in mind that spiritual growth is gradual. Consequently, we become more merciful as we are transformed into the image of Christ and should not be discouraged when we fall short. It is also true that some Christians have the spiritual gift of mercy and will display great mercy more often and at an earlier stage of Christian maturity. Just remember, regardless of our gifts and temperament, the grace of God is always available and sufficient for us to mature into a natural (according to our new nature) outflow of understanding, forbearance, and forgiveness toward the people we interact with on a daily basis. Our part is not to be perfect but to wholeheartedly agree what God says is true, to ask for His grace in every situation, and to depend on His strength and power to bring it to pass.

Mercy Is the Character of the Father

Our Heavenly Father is merciful, and we certainly would not want it any other way. For that matter, under the Mosaic Law, most of us would have been stoned for disobedience to our parents and would never have made it to adulthood. Apart from our covenant with Jesus Christ, we would still be under "the law of sin and death" (Romans 8:2)—with all of its consequences. God, in His mercy, sent His Son to shed His blood for our sin so we would "not [be] under law but under grace" (Romans 6:14)—partakers of the New Covenant.

> But You, O Lord, are a God merciful and gracious, Slow to anger and abundant in lovingkindness and truth. (Psalm 86:15)

Methuselah

Just one beautiful example of God's long-suffering and mercy is seen in the name Methuselah, which means, "he dies and it [the flood] is sent."[13] Methuselah lived longer than any person has ever lived. Another interesting fact about Methuselah is seen in Genesis 5:22. There, we are told, "Enoch walked with God three hundred years after he became the father of Methuselah." Although scripture does not explicitly state whether Enoch did or did not walk close to God before Methuselah was born, there is an inference that Methuselah's name may have inspired Enoch to walk with God.[14]

[13.] Fausset's Bible Dictionary, e-sword
[14.] John Wesley's Explanatory Notes, e-sword

Can you imagine what it would be like waking up each day with the awareness that when your son died, the earth would be destroyed with a flood? We do not have an account as to Enoch's understanding of how and why the flood would be sent. Moreover, it is safe to presume God did not inspire Enoch to name his son Methuselah if it had no meaning to him. However the exact details went, we do know after Methuselah was born, Enoch did walk with God and the year Methuselah died, the flood came.

This is an understated, yet beautiful, recording of the mercy and forbearance of God. Since God intended to flood the earth when Methuselah died, He lovingly waited 969 years before destroying mankind (apart from Noah and his family on the ark). Methuselah became the longest-living man. God bore the wickedness of mankind as long as He could before sending the flood. The Lord's mercy endures forever!

Defining Mercy

The book definition of "mercy" from the *1828 Webster's Dictionary*, which at the time it was written, included biblical references in its definition of words, depicts a beautiful picture of how mercy is the character of our Heavenly Father.

That benevolence, mildness or tenderness of heart which disposes a person to overlook injuries, or to treat an offender better than he deserves; the disposition that tempers justice, and induces an injured person to forgive trespasses and injuries, and to forbear punishment, or inflict less than law or justice will warrant. In this sense, there is perhaps no word in our language precisely synonymous with mercy. That which comes nearest to it is grace. It implies benevolence, tenderness, mildness, pity or compassion, and clemency, but exercised only towards offenders. Mercy is a distinguishing attribute of the Supreme Being.[15]

The first part of this definition of mercy speaks of a "mildness or tenderness of heart." A soft heart is pliable, and even as Christ was able to "sympathize with our weaknesses" (Hebrew 4:15), a mild, tender heart is more likely to be touched by the adverse circumstances in people's lives. Those with a tender heart are also less likely to think too highly of themselves and are much more likely to be filled with compassion, even as our Heavenly Father is.

With this thought in mind, we are sometimes prone to make judgments against people who have made a real mess of their lives and really don't seem to want to change or rise above their circumstances. Our attitude can really be helped by recalling—with great thanksgiving—the way we were raised and the gifts we were born with. Remember, if we were gifted with intelligence it is just that—a gift. If we accepted the Lord at a young age, it was because we were blessed by having someone model or show us the way of salvation. If we were not raised in impoverished surroundings, it was not of our own doing but the grace of God. If we practice good hygiene and have gracious social skills, most likely it is because we were part of a family that taught us such practices. If we are able to present ourselves well, speak effectively, and are educated—remember how this came to be!

By now, I trust you see my point and will reconsider your attitude toward those who don't have the gifts you have, as well as the blessings and opportunities you had. Even in the case of those who had great beginnings and have chosen to suffer loss due to their choices in life, a mild, tender heart will respond to God with great thanksgiving for the things we were spared from, rather than force God to judge us as we judge others. The bottom line is this, we expect and want to be treated by our Heavenly Father with great tenderness. If we desire to be treated this way, we must seek to be an expression of our Father's character, by being gentle and tenderhearted in our encounters with people each and every day.

[15.] Webster's 1828 Dictionary, e-sword

The definition of mercy goes on to say that mercy overlooks injuries and treats an offender better than deserved. Mercy forbears punishment and, when punishment must be rendered, will apply punishment less than the law or justice might require. One attribute of God that helps us to react this way is love. Even as "God is love" (1 John 4:8b), by walking in love, we too will be much more merciful. Additionally, in 1 Peter, we see that "love covers a multitude of sins."

> Above all, keep fervent in your love for one another, because love covers a multitude of sins. (1 Peter 4:8)

The love of God literally covers our sins so that no evidence, which would necessitate God's righteous judgment upon us, remains. Since our offense (what we sow) is seen through His love, the result is that we are treated better than we deserve. Even as we continue to 'injure' Him through our selfishness and disobedience, He forgives us. His infinite forbearance repeatedly gives us less than what we deserve. This is truly merciful, and "mercy is a distinguishing attribute of the Supreme Being."

Mercy vs. Grace

The *1828 Webster's Dictionary* definition goes on to explain there really is no English equivalent to the word "mercy," and the closest English word is actually "grace." When we try to apply the definitions of mercy and grace to our lives, it is common to confuse the meanings of the two words. For clarity, an often used and simple explanation of the difference between mercy and grace is: "Grace is receiving what we do not deserve from God; whereas mercy is not receiving what we do deserve."

With this definition in mind, for us to be merciful in our everyday lives, we need to ask the Lord for His strength to not respond to people according to what they deserve. As we allow the Lord to extend love and mercy through us to those in our daily lives—those who undeniably deserve otherwise—we certainly will be "peculiar people" (1 Peter 2:9, KJV) in this world.

It is important to note here, there will be times when the Lord seems to be leading us to respond to another person in a way that seems unmerciful. As humans, we tend to think mercy is giving a person what they want or, if we were in their place, what we would want. In God's foreknowledge, however, mercy may look like tragedy and trials in order to "discipline" (Hebrews 12:8) us or to spare us from "suffering loss." Since we would rarely choose to experience anything unpleasant or difficult ourselves, our tendency is to project what we would want into a situation dealing with someone else. For this reason, it is very important to seek the "will of God" for each scenario before we decide how we should respond.

> For though I caused you sorrow by my letter, I do not regret it; though I did regret it—for I see that that letter caused you sorrow, though only for a while—I now rejoice, not that you were made sorrowful, but that you were made sorrowful to the point of repentance; for you were made sorrowful according to the will of God, so that you might not suffer loss in anything through us. For the sorrow that is according to the will of God produces a repentance without regret, leading to salvation, but the sorrow of the world produces death. (2 Corinthians 7:8–10)

According to this text, when God permits an event in our lives that brings godly sorrow, it is an act of mercy. Since the Lord alone knows what is in the hearts and minds of people, only He can ultimately show us what is truly merciful at any particular time in a person's life.

Mercy truly is the character of the Father—possibly not our version of mercy but mercy from a divine perspective. As we seek to walk in His kingdom on earth, we, too, will be expressions of the mercy of God in the lives of the people we associate with each and every day.

Mercy Is a Superior Way of Life—God's Kind of Life!

As stated previously, mercy is also a superior way of life. It is medically proven that stress is a major cause of disease, lack of sleep, depression, and elevated anxiety. When we refuse to be merciful, we increase our stress levels—poisoning our own bodies with chemicals released from the turmoil in our souls. When we refuse to extend mercy for any reason—despite our best rationalization—the quality of our life is deeply affected.

> The merciful, kind, and generous man benefits himself [for his deeds return to bless him], but he who is cruel and callous [to the wants of others] brings on himself retribution. (Proverbs 11:17, AMPC)

Additionally, mercy is a superior way of life because it 'feels good.' As partakers of the "divine nature" (2 Peter 1:4), it is not 'natural' for us to respond to others contrary to our new nature, which was created in the image of Christ. Revenge really isn't sweet, and watching a person go through pain and distress because of our lack of mercy isn't fun.

> Treat others the same way you want them to treat you. If you love those who love you, what credit is that to you? For even sinners love those who love them. If you do good to those who do good to you, what credit is that to you? For even sinners do the same. If you lend to those from whom you expect to receive, what credit is that to you? Even sinners lend to sinners in order to receive back the same amount. But love your enemies, and do good, and lend, expecting nothing in return; and your reward will be great, and you will be sons of the Most High; for He Himself is kind to ungrateful and evil men. Be merciful, just as your Father is merciful. (Luke 6:31–36)

Even non-Christians treat people good when they feel like it or when they think the other person has a right to fair treatment. In contrast, the "sons of the Most High" are told to respond to others, not as they deserve but as we would want people—and ultimately our Heavenly Father—to respond to us!

CHAPTER 11

The Beatitudes:
What Kingdom Life Looks Like
Blessed Are the Pure in Heart

Blessed are the pure in heart, for they shall see God.
—Matthew 5:8

Through this study of the Beatitudes, a pattern developed I had never noticed before. Years ago, I originally did an in-depth study of the Beatitudes for a series of local television programs. Even with the extensive preparation I did for that series, I did not see then what I am about to share: the Beatitudes are actually progressive steps to sanctification or holiness.

The Beatitudes—Steps to Holiness

In Matthew 5:3, Jesus started 'The Sermon on the Mount' with "Blessed are the poor in spirit, for theirs is the Kingdom of Heaven." He was starting a teaching describing the "Kingdom of Heaven" with what we now know as the Beatitudes. The closer our daily experience is to the attributes the Beatitudes describe, the more our lives will exhibit what the Kingdom of Heaven should look like on earth.

With a clearer perspective of the Beatitudes—as progressive steps to holiness—the first step is becoming 'poor in spirit.' Being poor in spirit prepares us to acknowledge our inability to save ourselves and to see our need for a personal application of Christ's sacrifice. Since accepting Christ as Savior is the entrance into the Kingdom of Heaven, it is also the first—and absolutely necessary—step to holiness.

Once we are born again, the next step in sanctification is to see our need to be transformed into the image of Christ. As the attitudes and actions of our lives begin to grieve us, we will "mourn" over our carnal condition and seek the Lord for the power to be made new. We must always acknowledge the need for change before we are ready to go through the process of change.

The next crucial step in our spiritual growth is the revelation of how full of pride we really are. Since "God is opposed to the proud, but gives grace to the humble" (1 Peter 5:5), we will never experience true spiritual growth without genuine humility; and if it's not genuine, it's not humility! Pride is the most common legal ground through which the enemy attacks. We, as well as others in the body of Christ, suffer much loss and destruction because of the pride we allow to remain in our lives.

Humility, then, is the prerequisite for the next step in our spiritual maturity, which is an ever-increasing sense we can do nothing without Him. Jesus made our constant need for connection with and dependence on Him very clear in John 15.

I am the vine, you are the branches; he who abides in Me and I in him, he bears much fruit, for apart from Me you can do nothing. (John 15:5)

Our growing dependence on the Lord brings increased humility, and humility results in an ever-increasing hunger and thirst for righteousness. The more we make righteous choices, the more Christlike we will become.

With consistent death-blows to our pride, we develop a growing sense of our inability to produce anything spiritual from our own efforts and we become much more "merciful." As our understanding of our great need for the mercy of God increases, we become more prone to extend mercy to others and to recognize our own unrighteous judgments! This process of progressive sanctification results in our "hearts" becoming ever more "pure."

Matthew Henry once said, "True Christianity lives in the heart." Only the outworking of the life of Christ within us can produce a pure heart—a heart like Christ's. Purity of heart is one of the results of becoming Christlike from the inside out. As our flesh is renewed and our heart is purified, we will become more accurate representations of Christ in the earth.

At some point in the maturing process, our will is wholly given to the Lord and we sincerely desire nothing but His will. After the surrender of our will—even in the times when we fall short—the desire of our heart, above all else, will still be to please the Lord. This is the attitude of a pure heart. Our heart continues to be kept pure through our love for the Lord and through a corresponding, healthy fear of displeasing Him. By this time in our spiritual growth, we will have surrendered our personal agendas, as well as our conscious use of manipulation, control, and self-preservation. Since we are our own worst enemy, this is a great place to be!

Blessed Are the Pure in Heart

> Blessed [happy, enviably fortunate, and spiritually prosperous—possessing the happiness produced by the experience of God's favor and especially conditioned by the revelation of His grace, regardless of their outward conditions] are the pure in heart, for they shall see God! (Matthew 5:8, AMPC)

Just in case you don't think having a pure heart is important for your well-being, the Amplified version of Matthew 5:8 should settle the issue. As in the case of the other Beatitudes, Jesus opened the discussion of each with "Blessed." The *Amplified Bible* defines "blessed" as "happy, enviably fortunate, and spiritually prosperous."

Just imagine the impact we would have in the world around us if these three attributes were displayed in our everyday lives. When I say 'displayed,' I'm certainly not speaking of the tiresome, religious, outward show self-effort produces. There is a place in the heart of God where our entire life is governed by His life, in contrast to our self-effort. Remember, self-effort is the application of our own law, whereas His life flows from our innermost being.

> Watch over your heart with all diligence, For from it flow the springs of life. (Proverbs 4:23)

The life of Christ flows unhindered from a pure heart. This flow is compared to "rivers of living water" (John 7:38). We do not propel this living water, but we can hinder the flow of life from our innermost being.

Happiness, such as the world has never seen, will also flow from a pure heart. Such good fortune will come upon us that God will cause those in our sphere of influence to envy us (which is okay when it's not our desire nor from our own agenda—this is divine favor). Moreover, on top of all this, we will be spiritually prosperous, which in and of itself, will bring forth happiness and good fortune in our lives.

Watch Over Your Heart

Since the benefits of a pure heart are unparalleled, we really need to know how to guard our hearts. It is impossible to be in this world without the environment in which we live affecting the way we think, the choices we make, and our emotions. Again, from Proverbs 4:23, "Watch over your heart with all diligence."

We watch over our hearts by controlling what we allow ourselves to look at, what we listen to, what we talk about, what we read, and what we think about. Our inner man is affected by the input received from our five senses. In order to experience the blessings promised to the pure in heart, we will have to be very sensitive as to what influences we allow ourselves to be exposed to. The darker the environment in which we live and work, the more diligent we must be in watching over our hearts. Despite all this, it is comforting to remember God understands the hour in which we live, our past, our individual makeup, and all other hindrances that could affect the purity of our hearts. He will always be there with His grace—"the divine influence upon the heart and its reflection in the life"[16]—with all the power of His Spirit to cause us to overcome every obstacle we may ever face.

It is crucial for us to see anything that could defile our hearts as poisonous to our souls and as destructive to the quality of our lives. We have to learn to hate "even the garment polluted by the flesh" (Jude 1:23) in order to have the tenacity to fight the battle for a pure heart. Unless we watch over our hearts with the same diligence with which we would guard precious treasure, our hearts will likely become defiled. If our hearts become defiled, we will reap a decline in the quality of life in direct proportion to the corruption we allow in our hearts. Mark 7 records Jesus' admonition to us.

> That which proceeds out of the man, that is what defiles the man. For from within, out of the heart of men, proceed the evil thoughts, fornications, thefts, murders, adulteries, deeds of coveting and wickedness, as well as deceit, sensuality, envy, slander, pride and foolishness. All these evil things proceed from within and defile the man. (Mark 7:20–23)

Great wickedness proceeds from the hearts of mankind. It is important to remember, however, no matter how dark this world gets, we are each responsible for guarding the gate to our own heart. We are each held accountable before God for what we allow to influence our heart.

The apostle Paul gave a similar exhortation to Titus.

> To the pure, all things are pure; but to those who are defiled and unbelieving, nothing is pure, but both their mind and their conscience are defiled. (Titus 1:15)

---

16. Strong's Hebrew and Greek Dictionary

Defining "Pure"

The word "pure" in Matthew 5:8 comes from the Greek word *"katharos."* The connotation of *"katharos"* in this verse is, "pure as being cleansed."[17] In other words, as long as we are in these bodies, we will have to be actively involved in the perpetual cleansing of our hearts. Since there are many meanings for the word "heart" in scripture, our definition will be: "the part of us consisting of our soul and spirit."

The cleansing of our hearts is a two-part process. The first part happened instantaneously at new birth, and the second part of cleansing consists of a progressive application of all Christ did for us. The cleansing of our hearts is actually nothing less than sanctification. John Sanford has wonderful insight in describing this process. He says, "Inner healing is a misnomer. It is really sanctification, the application of the cross and blood and resurrection life of Jesus to whatever in history has not yet been redeemed."[18]

Although I'm not ready to quit using the term "inner healing," the powerful reality of applying the "cross and blood and resurrection life of Jesus" to whatever in us has not been redeemed, says it all. Sanctification is really this easy to understand! The difficulty lies in the practical application of the truths of who we are in Christ and what He did for us. Walking out these truths is a lifetime renewing of our mind, will, and emotions.

Two New Testament references that speak of "washing" in regards to sanctification are Ephesians 5:26 and Titus 3:5.

> So that He migh-t sanctify her, having cleansed her by the washing of water with the word, that He might present to Himself the church in all her glory, having no spot or wrinkle or any such thing; but that she would be holy and blameless. (Ephesians 5:26–27)

[17.] Vine's Complete Expository Dictionary of New Testament Words, e-sword
[18.] *Delivering Places.* John Sanford

> He saved us, not on the basis of deeds which we have done in righteousness, but according to His mercy, by the washing of regeneration and renewing by the Holy Spirit. (Titus 3:5)

Jesus instantaneously cleansed us at new birth "by the washing of water with the word," which is synonymous in meaning with "the washing of regeneration." At that same instant, the Holy Spirit made our human spirit alive and Jesus exchanged His righteous nature for our sinful nature. In this context, we are washed by the "Word" of God—as in Christ, Himself.

The part of the purification of our hearts received at new birth is known as our "position in Christ" or "positional truth." This phrase is used as this is the spiritual position of every true believer, regardless of his or her performance. Our "position in Christ" is that He has "seated us with Him in the heavenly places" (Ephesians 2:6). Additionally, because of what Christ did on our behalf, God the Father sees us as righteous as His Son.

Our part in the purifying of our hearts is to obey the revealed will of God for our lives on a day-to-day basis. A life of Christian discipline will facilitate knowing God, as well as knowing His will for our lives.

We need to study the bible daily, memorize and meditate on scriptures, have a lifestyle of worship, listen to Christian music (exclusively, I might add), spend time separated with the Lord (in the 'secret place' or soaking in His presence), regularly attend worship services and bible studies (including an accountability group), and practice walking in the presence of God and praying continually. As we do, we will be filled with truth that will transform us by renewing our minds. In this sense, we will be washed by the water of the word—the written word and the Living Word.

The process of applying and obeying the word of God in our everyday lives makes up our personal experience and is known as "experiential truth." Experiential truth is ours when the truth we believe manifests itself as a reality in our personal experience.

Beloved, now we are children of God, and it has not appeared as yet what we will be. We know that when He appears, we will be like Him, because we will see Him just as He is. And everyone who has this hope fixed on Him purifies himself, just as He is pure. (1 John 3:2–3)

The Power of a Pure Heart

Let us draw near with a sincere heart in full assurance of faith, having our hearts sprinkled clean from an evil conscience and our bodies washed with pure water. Let us hold fast the confession of our hope without wavering, for He who promised is faithful. (Hebrews 10:22–23)

There is great power in a pure heart. A pure heart produces a clear conscience, and a clear conscience results in confidence before God. On the contrary, any spots or blemishes left in our hearts give place for Satan to intimidate us or cause havoc in our lives.

In Ephesians 4:27, the apostle Paul exhorts us to not "give place to the devil." Satan knows our level of confidence, as well as our authority and power, depend on not only our understanding of our position in Christ but also on the purity of our hearts. His tactic is to accuse us of our shortcomings—whether inward or outward— attempting to cripple our confidence and leave us feeling condemned. Only the confidence that comes from having a pure heart gives no "place" for the enemy to take hold. Remember, having a pure heart is not achieving perfection but is continually choosing to walk a holy life (as described in earlier chapters).

For if our heart condemns us, God is greater than our heart, and knows all things. Beloved, if our heart does not condemn us, we have confidence toward God. (1 John 3:20–21, NKJV)

This verse speaks of times when our performance looks good, but the condition of our heart condemns us. This is the essence of hypocrisy. Hypocrisy is the state where our thoughts, actions, or words are contrary to what is in our heart. We can be aware of secret sins and attitudes that we have either not repented from or have not cared enough to take the necessary steps to be freed from. This condition of mixture in our hearts will cause our hearts to condemn us—and rightfully so.

As John declares, this condition of hypocrisy is ridiculous since God knows all things and is well aware of what is in our hearts. God sees every bit of remaining carnality, along with the knowledge of why we allow such things to remain untouched. In contrast, if our heart does not condemn us, our confidence before God will give us the power to not only live a holy life but to change the world in which we live.

> For thus says the Lord GOD, the Holy One of Israel: "In returning and rest you shall be saved; In quietness and confidence shall be your strength. (Isaiah 30:15, NKJV)

The Lord often brings the words of this verse to mind, "In quietness and confidence shall be your strength." If the Lord continually needs to remind me of my need for confidence—after walking this path for years—confidence is definitely important! In my personal experience, the main attack against my confidence has always been rejection. Due to the constant bombardment of rejection in my life—from the womb on—my life would be one of loss and devastation if it were not for the confidence I continually draw from the Lord.

Pay close attention to the words you are about to read! It makes no difference how intelligent you are, how attractive and polished you look, your position in life, your multiplied talents, or your wealth. In order for you to be who God intended you to be and to do what He has planned for you to do, you will need God-given confidence, which ignores the taunting of the accuser and propels you forward, no matter what the obstacles.

Our entire destiny rests on our confidence in Him—not only in God's ability but in our ability. In contrast to arrogance, this quiet confidence is the necessary foundation to victoriously walk through the adverse circumstances of life to God's expected end. If we will just step into the water, He will part the waters before us—step by step. If we will get out of the boat at His command, we will walk on water. If He sends us out against Goliath, Goliath will fall before us. If we raise the staff of His authority on the banks of the Red Sea, He will give us dry ground to walk on, as well as hand us the destruction of our enemies when we reach the other side. If we have confidence in the Lord's bidding, the dead will be raised to life, the blind will be healed, the lame will walk, and the dumb will speak!

On the other hand, without this confidence, the taunting from our flesh and the enemy may achieve its goal. We can easily be derailed by the fear of personal loss or danger and can allow the familiar friends of ridicule and failure to rob us of our "inheritance in the saints" (Ephesians 1:18). The voices within tell us what we cannot do and torment us with thoughts, such as, "What will people think?" They also offer numerous suggestions like, "play it safe" or "turn around and run." Then, if all the enemy's other attempts fail, the common nag of, "Who do you think you are?" may finally "put us in our place," succeeding in causing us to "fall short of the glory of God" (Romans 3:23). Always remember, the lies of the enemy are designed to tempt us to "lean on" our "own understanding" (Proverbs 3:5) rather than respond to what God is saying to our hearts.

The battle of overcoming these giants in our lives is not an easy process but is absolutely necessary to be faithful to our Heavenly Father and to our call. It has taken years for me to walk in consistent victory in the area of confidence. Moreover, even now, I know enough to be aware of the possibility of the daily temptation to draw back from my confidence in Him.

The Power Within

The full power of Christ cannot be expressed through us without knowing that God—in us—is greater than anything or anyone that stands before us. Accordingly, faith in His ability—in us—releases the power of God into our situation. The New Testament repeatedly declares the hopelessness of living the Christian life apart from God's strength. Two expressions of the apostle Paul's dependence on the power within him are found in Romans 8:31 and Colossians 1:29.

> What then shall we say to these things? If God is for us, who is against us? (Romans 8:31)

> For this purpose also I labor, striving according to His power, which mightily works within me. (Colossians 1:29)

Our faith in the power of God within us, along with the confidence of God's faithfulness to perform what He has promised, releases the flood of the power of God into every situation. Even if your confidence level is pretty low, don't be discouraged. Continue to allow the Lord to guide, heal, and grow you up to a hundredfold release of power.

> And the one on whom seed was sown on the good soil, this is the man who hears the word and understands it; who indeed bears fruit and brings forth, some a hundredfold, some sixty, and some thirty. (Matthew 13:23)

Great power results from having a pure heart and resting with confidence on the power of God within. With this in mind, "Let us draw near with a sincere heart in full assurance of faith, having our hearts sprinkled clean from an evil conscience and our bodies washed with pure water." The only way to walk "in quietness and confidence" is with a heart sprinkled clean from an evil conscience. When our conscience is clean, we will run to our Heavenly Father without fear of rejection and with full assurance that we will receive abundant grace for our present need. Remember, a pure heart is a source of great power!

> Therefore let us draw near with confidence to the throne of grace, so that we may receive mercy and find grace to help in time of need. (Hebrews 4:16)

Those with a Pure Heart

Both Psalm 24 and Psalm 15 describe characteristics of a pure heart. These psalms also testify to the favor of God and the blessings given to the pure in heart.

> Who may ascend into the hill of the LORD? And who may stand in His holy place? He who has clean hands and a pure heart, who has not lifted up his soul to falsehood And has not sworn deceitfully. He shall receive a blessing from the LORD And righteousness from the God of his salvation. (Psalm 24:3–5)

The Mountain of the Lord

Scripture often uses the allegory of a mountain to portray the Kingdom of God. Since the physical city of Jerusalem is on a hill, we often read in scripture of worshippers going up to Jerusalem or up to the mountain of the Lord. The term "Mount Zion" is used interchangeably with Jerusalem and is also a term for the people of God.

Picturing a mountain in your mind, think of the Kingdom of God as a mountain with a path that is very broad at the bottom but progressively narrows as it winds up and around the mountain. At the lower levels, the path is very easy to see and easy to follow. However, as the path nears the summit of the mountain, it narrows and eventually disappears (since few follow the path to the high altitudes). Continuing on from the level where the path ends, each step of the way must be made in total dependence on the Lord—one step at a time.

> He makes my feet like hinds' feet, and sets me on my high places. (2 Samuel 22:34)

There are many who start the journey of holiness but for many reasons fall by the wayside and fail to "press on toward the goal for the prize of the upward call of God in Christ Jesus" (Philippians 3:14). As the journey becomes harder and requires a fuller abandonment of self and a greater yielding to the Lord, many give up and go back to their old way of living the Christian life.

As Psalm 24 tells us, only those who have "clean hands and a pure heart" will be able to ascend and remain at the top of God's holy hill (or mountain). The remnant among the church—those who have not allowed falsehood or deceit to remain in their hearts—will be blessed of the Lord, receive divine approval, and be known as a righteous people. Psalm 15 adds to the benefits and description of those who are allowed to remain on God's holy hill.

> A Psalm of David. O LORD, who may abide in Your tent? Who may dwell on Your holy hill? He who walks with integrity, and works righteousness, and speaks truth in his heart. He does not slander with his tongue, nor does evil to his neighbor, Nor takes up a reproach against his friend; In whose eyes a reprobate is despised, But who honors those who fear the LORD; He swears to his own hurt and does not change. (Psalm 15:1–4)

Similarly, in Psalm 15, the psalmist includes the need for integrity, experiential righteousness, and honesty. He then adds that those on God's holy hill will not have a lifestyle of slander. *Webster's 1828 Dictionary* lists the definition of slander as: "a false tale or report maliciously uttered and tending to injure the reputation of another by lessening him in the esteem of his fellow citizens."

This is the dictionary definition of slander. Of great interest, however, is the meaning of the word translated "slanderers" in 1 Timothy 3:11 (NKJV). There, the word is used for, "those who are given to finding fault with the demeanor and conduct of others and spreading their innuendos and criticisms in the church."[19] This is dramatically confirmed by the Greek word from which the word translated as "slanderers" comes from. The original word in 1 Timothy 3:11 (NKJV) is *"diabolos,"* as in the Accuser of the Brethren himself—the Devil. Slander is a weapon used by Satan—one that uses members of the body of Christ to destroy itself. This cannot be the habit of those who desire to walk in holiness and purity of heart.

[19.] Vine's Complete Expository Dictionary of New Testament Words, e-sword

Another important character trait of the one who dwells on
God's holy hill is that a "reprobate" will be despised by the pure in
heart. This is strong language, but it is important to hate what God
hates. This is especially true in the context of a society and a professing church, which would never think anyone should be despised.
Why would God's word say such a thing?

A reprobate is one whose heart God cannot approve, and neither should we. The simplest definition of a reprobate is, "not standing the test, rejected."[20] The term was primarily applied to metals, as
in Isaiah 1:22.

Your silver has become dross, Your wine mixed with water.
(Isaiah 1:22, NKJV)

The refining of silver is a common analogy used in scripture. In
the refining process of precious metals, intense heat is applied to the
metal. The metal is heated until it liquefies, at which time the dross
rises to the surface. The dross is scooped off, leaving the purity of the
remaining metal of a finer quality than before the heat was applied.

When applying this verse to the human heart, all that remains
in a reprobate's heart is the dross or the part thrown away. This means
there is nothing pure remaining in this one's heart. In New Testament
terms, this means the reprobate is no longer, or never was, a believer in
Christ (since the life of Christ within a true believer gives value to the
heart—regardless of performance). In other words, there is nothing
in the reprobate heart worthy of restoration because no life is present.

Another picture of God refining us as silver is a reference in
Zechariah to the refining of God's people by fire—through which
only a remnant will stand.

And I will bring the third part through the fire, Refine them as silver is refined, And test them as gold is tested. They will call on My
name, And I will answer them; I will say, "They are My people,"
And they will say, "The LORD is my God." (Zechariah 13:9)

_____
[20.] ibid

The second analogy in this verse, "Your wine mixed with water," refers to the biblical comparison of wine with the life of Christ in the believer. Here, the wine is so watered down it no longer is the real thing. It no longer has the composition of wine. Its mixture makes it worthless and of no value. Applying this analogy to a reprobate's heart, the reprobate is one who—regardless of his/her profession—does not have real wine (the life of Christ) within.

The apostle Paul presents the position of the reprobate, which is the opposite of the pure in heart, very clearly in the first chapter of Romans.

> And even as they did not like to retain God in their knowledge, God gave them over to a reprobate mind, to do those things which are not convenient; Being filled with all unrighteousness, fornication, wickedness, covetousness, maliciousness; full of envy, murder, debate, deceit, malignity; whisperers, Backbiters, haters of God, despiteful, proud, boasters, inventors of evil things, disobedient to parents, Without understanding, covenant breakers, without natural affection, implacable, unmerciful: Who knowing the judgment of God, that they which commit such things are worthy of death, not only do the same, but have pleasure in them that do them. (Romans 1:28–32, KJV)

As we read this list of characteristics of the reprobate mind, it is easy to see why a reprobate is to be despised by the pure in heart and why—in contrast to despising a reprobate—we are to honor those who fear the Lord.

In the process of purifying our hearts, our flesh is separated from our spirit, allowing us to increasingly know the difference between what is of the flesh and what is of the spirit. Until that time, we will still be highly susceptible to the "sentimental spirit of the flesh and the world system." The world system is set up to control people by their emotions, and when they fail to go along with the sentiment of the majority, to further control them through rejection and condemnation. In order to maintain the purity of our hearts, we will have to be very aware of this dynamic.

The final characteristic of the pure in heart shown in Psalm 15 is: "He swears to his own hurt and does not change." God's remnant will be known for integrity. We will stand behind what we say or admit to what we have done—regardless of the consequences. No matter what the cost for integrity may be, we will be faithful to our word. In the rare cases where we fail from the weakness of our flesh or where it becomes impossible to keep our word, we must apologize and make any restitution necessary. The pure in heart will be expressions on this earth of their Father in Heaven.

The Pure in Heart Shall See God

There are several scriptures that speak of when, where, and how God may be seen. This Beatitude, however, speaks of God's special favor toward the pure in heart. "To see the face of one, or to be in the presence of any one, were terms among the Jews expressive of great favor."[21]

In order to see the king, one had to be ushered into his presence. It was a high honor to be allowed into the presence of kings and princes. The pure in heart shall live in the presence of their King, Jesus, in the New Jerusalem. Their cooperation with the Lord throughout the fire qualifies them to be His bride. They are very special to Him.

The term "seeing" God is also a Hebraism for "being able to experience, enjoy or to possess something or someone."[22] The pure in heart will be able to experience God as a close friend in ways other believers never will. They will enjoy Him at a depth few will ever know, and He will share the secrets of His heart with those He can trust.

We will "see" God move in our lives in direct proportion to the purity of our hearts. Since the pure in heart have become totally dependent on the Lord, they continually look to Him to "see" what He is going to do next on their behalf. God will never disappoint

---

[21.] Albert Barne's Notes on the Bible, e-sword
[22.] ibid

them, and they will "see" the Lord move in their lives because of their childlike dependence and intimate relationship with Him.

> For the eyes of the LORD move to and fro throughout the earth that He may strongly support those whose heart is completely His. (2 Chronicles 16:9a)

This is a beautiful picture. As we look to the Lord, His eyes are moving throughout the earth looking for us. He is looking for us to "strongly support" us in every physical, emotional, and spiritual need. He longs to lavish upon us all that He is for all we are not and all that He has, for our every need. The pure in heart will be "blessed" (happy, enviably fortunate, and spiritually prosperous—possessing the happiness produced by the experience of God's favor and especially conditioned by the revelation of His grace, regardless of their outward conditions). The pure in heart will be called the friends of God!

CHAPTER 12

The Beatitudes:
What Kingdom Life Looks Like
Blessed Are the Peacemakers

Blessed are the peacemakers, for they shall be called sons of God.
—Matthew 5:9

In the chapter on the blessedness of humility, we discussed how the ministry of the Holy Spirit makes the bible a living word and can reveal numerous applications for our lives from the same scripture. With this truth in mind, we will study several various meanings for the word "peacemaker."

The word "peacemaker" comes from a Greek word meaning "to make peace." Some of the connotations of this word include "to bring peace," "to reconcile," and "to be at peace." The literal meaning of the word in Matthew chapter 5 is, "to make peace." Ultimately, our job as "sons of God" is "to make peace," which in the highest sense, is to align the earth, the heavens, and mankind with God's original intent. The Kingdom of God brings peace to every situation when the people, places, or things involved are aligned with God's original intent for His creation.

The Garden of Eden was a prototype of God's original design. His plan was for the garden to be the perfect environment for the man He created. It was His intent for man's environment to be a place where He could come and interact with His creation. If we think of such interaction with God only happening in a far-off place called heaven, we need a change of mind in regards to heaven. Heaven is not "heaven" because of a specific location but is "heaven" due to the presence of God. The presence of God in Eden allowed the Father to fellowship with His creation. The increase of His presence on earth will bring the atmosphere of "heaven" to earth, which will eventually make "all things new."

> And He who sits on the throne said, "Behold, I am making all things new." And He said, "Write, for these words are faithful and true." (Revelation 21:5)

Traditionally, the church has thought God would make "all things new" instantaneously, at one point in time. As the Lord gives increased revelation as to how scripture applies to the days in which we are living, however, we have a new understanding of how this will transpire. In the days of transition between the Church Age and the Lord's kingdom on earth, Father's intent is to make a new heaven and a new earth—by the fire of His glory, or His presence, in a chosen people.

> But by His word the present heavens and earth are being reserved for fire, kept for the day of judgment and destruction of ungodly men. (2 Peter 3:7)

> The day of the Lord's return will surprise us like a thief. The heavens will disappear with a loud noise, and the heat will melt the whole universe. Then the earth and everything on it will be seen for what they are. (2 Peter 3:10, CEV)

God has been waiting for 6,000 years for a generation to so fully express the image of His Son, that God in Christ would again walk the earth in the flesh—our flesh. As Christ is allowed to manifest Himself in the "sons of God," they will "make peace" through the release of the glory of God in their lives. In the first part of Christ's "appearing" (Titus 2:13), the intent of the fire of His presence will be to burn away all that is carnal in His church.

> Each man's work will become evident; for the day will show it because it is to be revealed with fire, and the fire itself will test the quality of each man's work. (1 Corinthians 3:13)

> For it is time for judgment to begin with the household of God; and if it begins with us first, what will be the outcome for those who do not obey the gospel of God? (1 Peter 4:17)

When the chaff is removed, "then the earth and everything on it will be seen for what they are." As "the thoughts and intentions of the heart" (Hebrews 4:12) are revealed, we will have the opportunity to respond with repentance or to harden our hearts. Since this may be God's last warning for many professing believers, the Lord—in His love—will bring conviction with great intensity. The Lord will no longer be 'winking' at hearts that choose lifestyles or choices contrary to His direct leading. This is not speaking of the process of falling and picking ourselves up as we are conformed to His image but of habitual and willful disobedience.

For believers who continually harden their hearts by deliberately making choices contrary to the clear, known will of the Lord, there will be 'conviction with consequence.' Conviction with consequence means that hardening our hearts to the conviction of the Holy Spirit may eventually result in quick and sudden judgment in our personal lives. "God is not mocked" will have new meaning in "the day of vengeance of our God" (Isaiah 61:2).

This divine intervention—not typically seen before this time—will be God's last attempt to spare us from the many ramifications of falling "short of the glory of God" (Romans 3:23). The judgment that will come upon the church might seem extreme to us but, in reality, is an expression of the love of God for His beloved. We really do not understand the putrid condition of the church at large. We could compare ourselves to Lot's wife living in Sodom and Gomorrah. She had become so acclimated to the deplorable moral conditions around her that she had no desire to leave. The church of Jesus Christ is presently in such a state of carnality. Our only hope of being transformed from the description of the church at Laodicea (Revelation 3:14-22) into His bride is divine intervention. The intent of this conviction and possible consequential judgment is to be an example to wayward believers—in order to restore the fear of the Lord in His church and to spare believers from the "wrath to come" (1 Thessalonians 1:10) through repentance. The bible refers to the time period we are describing as "the day of the Lord."

> For you yourselves know full well that the day of the Lord will come just like a thief in the night. While they are saying, "Peace and safety!" then destruction will come upon them suddenly like labor pains upon a woman with child, and they will not escape. (1 Thessalonians 5:2–3)

Many in the church are expecting to be raptured from the earth before this happens. Nonetheless, this belief will not stop "the day of the Lord" from coming. For those with this anticipation, His "appearing" will be "just like a thief in the night."

As He appears with ever-increasing glory through His overcoming army, most will not recognize His coming. Similarly, much of the church will not recognize His second coming—His "appearing"—in a multimembered body of mostly unknown, unimpressive overcomers. Jesus did not come the first time as His people (the Jews) expected. Consequently, most of them failed to recognize the "time of their visitation" (Luke 19:41–44) and missed their opportunity to be a part of His eternal plan. Even so in our day, due to the spiritual complacency of the church, many will ignore the conviction and warnings of the Lord as they say, "Peace and safety!"

Those who do not recognize His "appearing" and, as a result, do not judge themselves—so they will "not be judged" (1 Corinthians 11:31)—will be allowed to go their own way. In the exercise of their freewill, many will choose the immediate gratification of their flesh over repentance, resulting in the great "falling away" (2 Thessalonians

2:13, KJV). Although, "The Lord is not slow about His promise, as some count slowness, but is patient toward you, not wishing for any to perish but for all to come to repentance" (2 Peter 3:9), there comes a time when our "visitation" is over, and God's plan must move forward. The scriptures are clear that "the day of the Lord" must come. The Church Age will draw to a close as the Kingdom Age begins. It is our choice, however, as to whether we will pay the price to be a part of what is to come. The Lord has promised "new heavens and a new earth, in which righteousness dwells," and all of His promises will be fulfilled.

> But according to His promise we are looking for new heavens and a new earth, in which righteousness dwells. Therefore, beloved, since you look for these things, be diligent to be found by Him in peace, spotless and blameless. (2 Peter 3:13–14)

Peace in Sanctification

It is of note, "peace" is placed in a verse that speaks of "a new earth, in which righteousness dwells." It is also significant that it proceeds "spotless and blameless." The truth is, there really is no peace apart from being "spotless and blameless." True sanctification brings peace. The depth of our peace will always be a barometer of our spiritual growth.

> The work of righteousness will be peace, And the effect of righteousness, quietness and assurance forever. (Isaiah 32:17, NKJV)

Ultimately, we are called to make peace by bringing all things into alignment with God's original intent. In addition, a peacemaker "connects into one."[23] To the highest degree, "connecting into one" is to cooperate with the purposes of God in bringing the bride into union with her bridegroom, Who is Jesus.

[23.] Adam Clarke's Commentary on the Bible, e-Sword, Matthew 5:9

For this reason, we are called to proclaim the message of our co-crucifixion with Christ and the need to lay down our life for His. Union with Christ, which will result in union with each other, is the goal we press toward and the only solution for true peace. On a vertical plane, we have peace with God through the restoration of unity with His Son, which gives us one object and one interest—His will. On a horizontal plane, we will have peace with each other as the "unity of the Spirit" is restored.

> Being diligent to preserve the unity of the Spirit in the bond of peace. (Ephesians 4:3)

True unity—outworking from the grace of God—will also give us one corporate objective and interest. This unity cannot be manufactured by man through any program or legislation but is a supernatural byproduct of union with Christ and with each other.

A peacemaker also "labors for the public good and feels his own interest promoted in promoting that of others."[24] This thought is reminiscent of the blessedness of humility. When we serve others, we esteem them higher than ourselves. Serving others above our own interests will also promote peace.

> If possible, so far as it depends on you, be at peace with all men. (Romans 12:18)

Instead of "fanning the fire of strife," a peacemaker "uses his influence and wisdom to reconcile the contending parties, adjust their differences and restore them to a state of unity. As all men are represented to be in a state of hostility to God and each other, the Gospel is called the Gospel of peace, because it tends to reconcile men to God and to each other."[25]

[24.] ibid
[25.] ibid

> Now all these things are from God, who reconciled us to Himself through Christ and gave us the ministry of reconciliation, namely, that God was in Christ reconciling the world to Himself, not counting their trespasses against them, and He has committed to us the word of reconciliation. Therefore, we are ambassadors for Christ, as though God were making an appeal through us; we beg you on behalf of Christ, be reconciled to God. (2 Corinthians 5:18–20)

Our Father, Who is the "God of peace," has given us "the ministry of reconciliation." We will not have peace with God, internal peace, or true peace with each other until we have been reconciled to Him.

> Now may the God of peace Himself sanctify you entirely; and may your spirit and soul and body be preserved complete, without blame at the coming of our Lord Jesus Christ. (1 Thessalonians 5:23)

When Jesus charged His disciples to "go into all the world and preach the gospel to all creation" (Mark 16:15), it was a charge to preach the need for mankind's reconciliation with God. Apart from an acceptable sacrifice, Adam and Eve's sin cost them and their descendants (all of mankind) eternal life, as well as the ability to fellowship with God. In the Father's eternal plan, however, Jesus came as an acceptable, 'once-for-all' sacrifice, restoring the hope of eternal life and the possibility of intimate fellowship with the Father. Hence, "to make peace" is to also proclaim the message of the availability of reconciliation with the God of the universe through His Son, Jesus Christ. Reconciliation with God brings the possibility of increasing levels of internal peace—through peace with God.

Ambassadors of Peace

The last meaning of "peacemaker" comes from the classic Greek usage of the word, where a peacemaker was an ambassador sent to make a peace treaty.[26] Applying this meaning to Matthew 5:9, "a better rendering of the Greek word would be "peace workers," implying not merely making peace between those who are at variance but working peace which is the will of the God of peace for men."[27]

We typically think of God as love because "God is love" (1 John 4:8), but He is also the "God of peace." In fact, God is every facet of His character the bible expresses. He is every "fruit of the Spirit" (Galatians 5:22) because the Holy Spirit is God. God is love; He is joy, peace, patience, kindness, goodness, and faithfulness. He is the essence of every good thing, and apart from Him all else is counterfeit. "God is not the author of confusion but of peace" (1 Corinthians 14:33), which means He is the "author of peace." True peace begins with Him and emanates only from Him.

Sons of God

In the context of this chapter, we need to remember we have been left on this earth as ambassadors of the "God of peace" in order to bring peace to the earth as carriers of His life. Only "sons of God" are qualified to be ambassadors of God on the earth. In the most basic sense, all who have received Christ as Savior are children of God and thus "sons of God."

> For you are all sons of God through faith in Christ Jesus. (Galatians 3:26)

Although this is true, we will only be able to represent God on the earth to the degree we are expressions of His likeness. For this reason, in order to be accurate representatives of God, we must yield to and obey the Spirit of God within us. We know our flesh cannot maintain trying to be Christlike, but will eventually break down in any attempt at holiness. However, when the Spirit is leading us, our lives will begin to represent Christ on the earth.

[26.] International Standard Bible Encyclopedia, e-Sword
[27.] ibid

190

For all who are being led by the Spirit of God, these are sons of God. (Romans 8:14)

As a result of being "led by the Spirit of God," the "sons of God" will be "those who resemble God or who manifest a spirit like His."[28]

In Genesis 6:2, there is an account of the "sons of God" taking the "daughters of men" as wives. There have been many explanations offered as to who the sons of God in this text are. Several historical writers and bible commentators agree, however, the Genesis reference most likely refers to these men as sons of God because they were men who followed God or resembled God.

In this example, the offspring of Seth were called sons of God because they resembled God. The descendants of Seth lived in the mountain region and compromised their walk with God by inter-marrying with the ungodly offspring of Cain, who lived in the valley below. In order for us to be known as those who "resemble God" or "manifest a spirit like His," we cannot do as the descendants of Seth but must be diligent to be uncompromising in following our Lord.

The late A.B. Simpson penned a beautiful expression of this truth in his devotional *Days of Heaven on Earth*:

God wants us here on this earth for some higher purpose than mere existence. That purpose is to represent Him to the world, to be the messengers of His gospel and His will to men and women, and by our lives to exhibit to them the true life and teach them how to live it. He is repre-senting us in heaven, and our one business is to represent Him on earth. We are just as truly sent into this world to represent Him as if we had gone to China as the ambas-sador of the United States government. Although we may be engaged in the secular affairs of life, it is simply that we may represent Christ here, carry on His business and use our means to further His cause.[29]

28. Albert Barne's Notes on the Bible. e-Sword
29. *Days of Heaven on Earth*. A.B. Simpson, December 31

In the last days, there will be an additional significance to the term "sons of God"—unique to any other time in history. The designation will still include those who have trusted in Jesus as their Savior and those who manifest a spirit like His and, as a result, resemble Him. However, in addition to these definitions, in the time of transition between the Church Age and the Kingdom Age, the Lord will have an overcoming army on the earth, who will be called the sons of God.

> For the anxious longing of the creation waits eagerly for the revealing of the sons of God. For the creation was subjected to futility, not willingly, but because of Him who subjected it, in hope that the creation itself also will be set free from its slavery to corruption into the freedom of the glory of the children of God. For we know that the whole creation groans and suffers the pains of childbirth together until now. And not only this, but also we ourselves, having the first fruits of the Spirit, even we ourselves groan within ourselves, waiting eagerly for our adoption as sons, the redemption of our body. (Romans 8:19–23)

Creation will only be released from the curse of sin at one time in history, and this will be when the heavens and earth are made new. The "creation" is waiting "eagerly for the revealing of the sons of God" since they will be the vessels God uses to release His purifying fire (glory) on the earth. This fire will begin the process of reversing the effects of sin in the earth.

> Behold, I am going to send My messenger, and he will clear the way before Me. And the Lord, whom you seek, will suddenly come to His temple; and the messenger of the covenant, in whom you delight, behold, He is coming," says the LORD of hosts. "But who can endure the day of His coming? And who can stand when He appears? For He is like a refiner's fire and like fullers' soap. He will sit as a smelter and purifier of silver, and He will purify the sons of Levi and refine them like gold

and silver, so that they may present to the LORD offerings in righteousness. Then the offering of Judah and Jerusalem will be pleasing to the LORD as in the days of old and as in former years. (Malachi 3:1–4)

Prepare the Way of the Lord

The Hebrew word for "messenger" can be used for an angel but is also used for an ambassador or prophet. The "sons of God" will be ambassadors of God, ministering in the spirit of the prophets who have gone before them. In the spirit of John the Baptist, one main task will be to "prepare the way of the Lord."

> In those days John the Baptist came preaching in the wilderness of Judea, and saying, "Repent, for the Kingdom of Heaven is at hand!" For this is he who was spoken of by the prophet Isaiah, saying: "The voice of One crying in the wilderness: 'Prepare the way of the Lord; Make His paths straight.'" (Matthew 3:1–3, NKJV)

As messengers of God sent before the physical return of the Lord, the sons of God will be sent to the church (Judah and Jerusalem). They will "prepare the way of the Lord" by calling for repentance and for the purification of the bride. Their message will be, "the Kingdom of Heaven is at hand." This will be the last chance for the church to purify herself before the "door" is "shut" (Matthew 25:10) to the marriage supper of the Lamb. After the consummation of the marriage, the purified bride—made up of the overcoming army and those from the church that have rightly responded to the Lord's purification process—will then go forth to reap the end time harvest.

Kings and Priests

Looking back at Romans chapter 8, the earth is now waiting for freedom from the results of sin. At the same time, the "children of God" are waiting for "the redemption of" the "body." Both will come as a result of the second coming of the Lord during the closing out of the Church Age and the setting up of His kingdom on earth. Beginning at this time of transition, the sons of God will be used by God both as kings (or rulers in His kingdom) and as priests on the earth.

> And He has made us to be a kingdom, priests to His God and Father—to Him be the glory and the dominion forever and ever. Amen. (Revelation 1:6)

> And hath made us kings and priests unto God and his Father; to him be glory and dominion for ever and ever. Amen. (Revelation 1:6, KJV)

Some versions of this text, including the KJV, read "kings and priests" rather than "made us to be a kingdom." Nonetheless, both will be true of the overcomers. As overcomers, we are both a part of the kingdom Jesus brought to earth through His incarnation and "kings" or rulers in this kingdom.

As part of the 'job description' of "kings," the Lord will place the sons of God in positions of authority in His kingdom. Initially, before the earthly kingdom of the Lord is established, this authority will be spiritual in nature. Scripture does not give us too many details as to what our earthly reign with the Lord will look like, but scripture is clear that we will rule and reign with Christ.

> If we endure, we will also reign with Him; If we deny Him, He also will deny us. (2 Timothy 2:12)

> He who overcomes, and he who keeps My deeds until the end, To him I will give authority over the nations; and he shall rule them with a rod of iron, as the vessels of the potter are broken to pieces, as I also have received authority from My Father. (Revelation 2:26–27)

He who overcomes, I will grant to him to sit down with Me on My throne, as I also overcame and sat down with My Father on His throne. (Revelation 3:21)

You have made them to be a kingdom and priests to our God; and they will reign upon the earth. (Revelation 5:10)

Then I saw thrones, and they sat on them, and judgment was given to them. And I saw the souls of those who had been beheaded because of their testimony of Jesus and because of the word of God, and those who had not worshiped the beast or his image, and had not received the mark on their forehead and on their hand; and they came to life and reigned with Christ for a thousand years. (Revelation 20:4)

Blessed and holy is the one who has a part in the first resurrection; over these the second death has no power, but they will be priests of God and of Christ and will reign with Him for a thousand years. (Revelation 20:6)

And there will no longer be any night; and they will not have need of the light of a lamp nor the light of the sun, because the Lord God will illumine them; and they will reign forever and ever. (Revelation 22:5)

The movie, *The Chronicles of Narnia: The Lion, the Witch and the Wardrobe*, gives us a visual expression of the preceding verses. In the movie, Aslan—the lion who represents Jesus—returns to Narnia, overcomes the powers of darkness, and sets up his kingdom. At that time, he crowns the offspring of Adam and gives them thrones and authority over specific geographic areas. Even though this is just C. S. Lewis' interpretation of what ruling and reigning with Christ might look like, at the least, it stirs our imagination and helps us visualize just a part of the magnificence of what the Lord has in store for those who overcome for love of their Master.

Prior to the time when the Kingdom of Heaven is established on earth, our spiritual authority will be exercised through declaration and intercession. In the closing out of the Church Age, the Lord will use the overcoming army to "patrol the heavenlies."[30] As we spend greater and greater time in the presence of the Lord, we will cultivate an increased spiritual sensitivity. This sensitivity will give us the ability to discern His will and hear His voice, even during our everyday routines. We will then be able to release or speak forth (whether audibly or in our heads) the will of the Lord at any time of day or night.

There will still be times of corporate prayer and intercession, however, the Lord is training an army that will walk this world as He did—unknown, unrecognized, and seemingly powerless—until the revealing of the bride. During this transitional period, we may be given authority in the heavenlies for specific physical territories, but much of our reigning with Christ will be in secret. As we show ourselves faithful to seek Him until we know His will and His words and then are obedient to "the counsel of His will" (Ephesians 1:11), we will be trusted with greater authority. We will also be given authority in proportion to our willingness to suffer for Him (as we obey His known will to the best of our revelation and ability).

> That I may know Him and the power of His resurrection and the fellowship of His sufferings, being conformed to His death. (Philippians 3:10)

Through the 'job description' of "priests" in the kingdom, we will be instruments of peace on the earth by ministering unto God. Jesus absolutely became the only sacrifice for our sins—past, present, and future—we will ever need. However, as priests under the new covenant, one sacrifice the Lord would still have us offer to Him is our life as a living sacrifice. In contrast to the typical, old covenant sacrifice, a living sacrifice was brought to the temple to be used by the priests of the Lord for as long as it lived. The twelfth chapter of

---

[30.] *The Corporate Man* (on CD). Graham Cooke

Romans tells us that offering our lives as a living sacrifice is an act of worship to our Lord.

> Therefore I urge you, brethren, by the mercies of God, to present your bodies a living and holy sacrifice, acceptable to God, which is your spiritual service of worship. (Romans 12:1)

The phrase "your spiritual service of worship" tells us that offering ourselves as a living sacrifice, which necessitates the relinquishing of all our rights, is the least we can do for our Lord—apart from Whom we would have nothing. Thus, in our role as priests unto the Lord, we will continually worship the Lord through the offering up of our very lives.

There is a seldom-referenced scripture in Malachi that gives insight as to how the sons of God will minister as priests in the kingdom. In reference to the tribe of Levi (the tribe of Israel that served as the Old-Testament priests), God relates the covenant He made with Levi.

> My covenant with him was one of life and peace, and I gave them to him as an object of reverence; so he revered Me and stood in awe of My name. True instruction was in his mouth and unrighteousness was not found on his lips; he walked with Me in peace and uprightness, and he turned many back from iniquity. For the lips of a priest should preserve knowledge, and men should seek instruction from his mouth; for he is the messenger of the LORD of hosts. (Malachi 2:5–7)

As we maintain the heart attitude of a living sacrifice, as priests in His kingdom, the Lord will extend "life and peace" to us. We will be known as those who carry the life and will be sought out for all the life of the Lord offers to an individual. Similarly, as the Lord fills us with peace, we will overflow peace into our surroundings. This peace will be one fruit of the Spirit that will draw men unto the Lord. As the days in which we live grow increasingly dark and unpredictable, the supernatural peace we will walk in will be the trademark of the overcomer.

The next attribute of the overcomer seen in the Malachi text is that "true instruction" will be in our mouths and "unrighteousness" will not be found on our lips. As the body of Christ, we are His representatives or, as we have said previously, His ambassadors. The words of life will be on our lips, and the Living Word inside us will be able to express Himself through our mouths. This will bring an authority in the words we speak similar to the authority Christ had as He walked the earth. One of the major accusations from the Jewish leaders of His time was that He spoke as one who had authority, which threatened their authority (Matthew 7:28–29).

As the world has become darker and darker, we have seen that integrity is a rare character trait. Proportionally then, the darker the world becomes, the more integrity will be a rare jewel and will be another trademark of the overcomer. Due to its scarcity, integrity—even as peace—will draw the world to the Lord as people long for something or someone they can trust.

As the Lord originally intended for the tribe of Levi, we will walk the earth with the Lord in "peace and uprightness." As a result of our overcoming life, many will be "turned...back from iniquity" and will be spared the wrath of those who "fall short of the glory of God" (Romans 3:23). We will truly be accurate messengers of the Lord and will "preserve" the true "knowledge" of the Lord in times of confusion and perversity.

The Reward of the Peacemakers

"Blessed are the peacemakers, for they shall be called sons of God." There is great reward for being a peacemaker. "Peacemakers" are "blessed" or, as one amplification for "blessed" from the *Amplified Bible* reads, "spiritually prosperous." As we seek to be peacemakers, spiritual prosperity will be our reward, spiritual prosperity will enable us to overcome, and as overcomers we will "be called sons of God." As "sons of God," we will reign with our Lord—working hand in hand with Him as "fellow heirs."

And if children, heirs also, heirs of God and fellow heirs with Christ, if indeed we suffer with Him so that we may also be glorified with Him. (Romans 8:17)

In this process, we will experience an eternity beyond our wildest dreams. No matter what your present circumstances are, think of what the Lord has in store for those who overcome and press on for "the joy set before" you!

Fixing our eyes on Jesus, the author and perfecter of faith, who for the joy set before Him endured the cross, despising the shame, and has sat down at the right hand of the throne of God. (Hebrews 12:2)

CHAPTER 13

The Beatitudes:
What Kingdom Life Looks Like
Blessed Are the Persecuted

Blessed and happy and enviably fortunate and spiritually prosperous (in the state in which the born-again child of God enjoys
and finds satisfaction in God's favor and salvation, regardless
of his outward conditions) are those who are persecuted for
righteousness' sake (for being and doing right), for theirs is the
Kingdom of Heaven! Blessed (happy, to be envied, and spiritually prosperous—with life-joy and satisfaction in God's favor
and salvation, regardless of your outward conditions) are you
when people revile you and persecute you and say all kinds
of evil things against you falsely on My account. Be glad and
supremely joyful, for your reward in heaven is great (strong and
intense), for in this same way people persecuted the prophets
who were before you.

—Matthew 5:10–12 (AMPC)

I originally started out using the *New American Standard Bible*
for this text. Upon reading these verses in the classic edition of the
Amplified Bible, however, I was energized to write this chapter—just
from reading the key text! Let's face it, most of us are not excited

about persecution. Yet, whether it is because of the time in which we live or due to an ever-increasing understanding of the last day army of the Lord, I read the word "persecuted" with less fear and trepidation than I have at any other time in life. My hope is that after reading this chapter, you will also share in my newfound freedom.

I have always been, and still am, very compliant and obedient, so as to not face the painful alternatives. The Lord has brought me from the child/woman who played it safe, to a warrior just waiting for my Commander's next order. In fact, I'm sure my eyes twinkle at the thought of battle. After all, the Lord has clearly promised if we endure to the end, we will win—whether in the body or out of the body!

At this point, it might help to reiterate just what a Christian is and why we are left on this earth after being born again. We are a spirit, who has a soul (mind, will, and emotions), and lives in a body. In reference to our body, Bill Gillham coined the term "earthsuit"[31] from the late C.S. Lovett (since the earth is the only place we will ever need this body). The purpose of our existence on earth is to be conformed to the image of Christ through "the fellowship of His sufferings" (Philippians 3:10) and through intimacy with God—until our union with Christ is experiential, as well as positional. When the eyes of our heart become adjusted to looking above, rather than looking at our surroundings here on earth (Colossians 3:1–2), the circumstances around us will have less and less of a downward pull. As we cultivate the practice of walking in the presence of the Lord, with our mind on Him, the pull of the cares and concerns of this life will continue to weaken.

In regards to persecution, our dread usually comes from a fear of death. Personally, I've never feared death. What has made me uneasy at times, however, was the thought of the pain I could suffer on the way out or, worse yet, the condition I could be left in if I happened to live. I really don't like pain!

For those of you who fear death, I purposely used the last paragraph to set the stage for the following word picture. As a Christian

---

[31.] Bill Gillham. *Lifetime Guarantee.* Pg. 147

walking close to the Lord, when we take our last breath, our inner man—spirit and soul—will leave this body made of dirt and will instantly be in the presence of the Lord. The more detached we are from the things of earth and the closer our walk with God, the less eventful this transition will be. In fact, it could be as uneventful as leaving one room in a house and walking into the next. It may even take us a while to realize we are finally free from the limitations of our earthly body!

I am making a point of sharing these things so you can have a chance for a new perspective on death and suffering. People pay massive amounts of money to go on extreme sport adventures, remote hunting expeditions, or dangerous vacations to exciting places, but there are few who get excited about 'throwing caution to the wind' for Christ. I truly have decided that whatever my future holds, I am going on with gusto for God. This is a much more fulfilling life—far greater in experience and of incomprehensible worth when compared to any earthly substitute. What do we have to lose? After all, it's not what you go through in life but how you go through it!

The Persecuted Really Are Blessed
Regardless of Outward Conditions

The key text contains the phrase "in the state in which the born-again child of God enjoys and finds satisfaction in God's favor and salvation, regardless of his outward conditions." The emphasis on "regardless of his outward conditions" is found in all but two of the Beatitudes in the *Amplified Bible*. I believe the significance of this phrase in the original language (which is what is explained in the parenthesis in the *Amplified Bible*) is that if we are to experience the blessings promised in the Beatitudes, our focus must be on the kingdom within us rather than the turmoil around us.

As Christians, we tend to look at outward circumstances as indicators of being blessed, favored by God, or whether we are walking in the will of God. With the propensity to focus on the outward, we can easily miss the 'real thing.' Since the Kingdom of God is an invisible kingdom within us, our peace, joy, and contentment must flow from an inward satisfaction that what God says is true—regardless of our experience at the time.

As of late, the Lord has been emphasizing the same truth over and over again to my heart: "Things are not as they seem but how I make them." As we look at the decaying world around us, we must never forget God is in control and nothing touches us apart from the lifting of His hand. We must also remember, "God causes all things to work together for good to those who love God" (Romans 8:28). He miraculously and consistently works in ways beyond our understanding! When something 'bad' comes into our lives, God touches it (no matter how terrible it is) and uses it for our 'good.' Becoming good for us does not mean the circumstances change or that the 'bad' results are reversed. Nonetheless, when we receive the bad with thanksgiving—as allowed by God—He always uses it to better our lives.

> In everything give thanks; for this is God's will for you in Christ Jesus. (1 Thessalonians 5:18)

Acceptance with thanksgiving is the real key to resetting our internal 'feeler gauges'—to feel blessed even when persecuted. No matter what our outward conditions look like, we must train ourselves to immediately acknowledge God's love for us and His supreme control over our lives. We must thank Him for what, ultimately, He allowed to touch us. When we do this, we release the atmosphere of heaven into our situation and permit God to work all things together for our good. Until the King, Himself, touches this earth and sets up His earthly kingdom, we will have tribulation.

> These things I have spoken to you, so that in Me you may have peace. In the world you have tribulation, but take courage; I have overcome the world. (John 16:33)

It is fundamental for us to understand that just because we are Christians, we may not always be shielded from trouble. This is planet Earth, not Heaven, and God is not Santa Claus. All of us—

born again and not born again—will have tribulation in this world. Albeit, since Jesus has overcome the world, we can choose to let Him overcome in us.

> But I say to you, love your enemies, and pray for those who persecute you in order that you may be sons of your Father who is in heaven; for He causes His sun to rise on the evil and the good, and sends rain on the righteous and the unrighteous. (Matthew 5:44–45)

Terrible things happen in this imperfect world, but we have a Heavenly Father who saves our tears in a bottle and knows the number of hairs on our heads—nothing takes Him by surprise. The promises in His word were written to give peace and encouragement to His children during the extremely difficult times of life. We would have no need for supernatural peace if we were always exempted from affliction.

> Therefore we do not lose heart, but though our outer man is decaying, yet our inner man is being renewed day by day. For momentary, light affliction is producing for us an eternal weight of glory far beyond all comparison, while we look not at the things which are seen, but at the things which are not seen; for the things which are seen are temporal, but the things which are not seen are eternal. (2 Corinthians 4:16–18)

But I Don't Deserve It

One of the hardest things for mankind to bear is persecution when we're 'doing what is right.' Our self-righteousness just can't stand being treated badly when we know we're 'being good.' It will often flare into a tirade that robs us of abundant life and—if left unchecked—can leave an opening for demonic oppression for years to come.

For this finds favor, if for the sake of conscience toward God a person bears up under sorrows when suffering unjustly. For what credit is there if, when you sin and are harshly treated, you endure it with patience? But if when you do what is right and suffer for it you patiently endure it, this finds favor with God. (1 Peter 2:19–20)

If you are reviled for the name of Christ, you are blessed, because the Spirit of glory and of God rests on you. Make sure that none of you suffers as a murderer, or thief, or evildoer, or a troublesome meddler; but if anyone suffers as a Christian, he is not to be ashamed, but is to glorify God in this name. (1 Peter 4:14–16)

But even if you should suffer for the sake of righteousness, you are blessed. And do not fear their intimidation, and do not be troubled, but sanctify Christ as Lord in your hearts, always being ready to make a defense to everyone who asks you to give an account for the hope that is in you, yet with gentleness and reverence; and keep a good conscience so that in the thing in which you are slandered, those who revile your good behavior in Christ will be put to shame. For it is better, if God should will it so, that you suffer for doing what is right rather than for doing what is wrong. For Christ also died for sins once for all, the just for the unjust, so that He might bring us to God, having been put to death in the flesh, but made alive in the spirit. (1 Peter 3:14–18)

As you read these verses, notice God's reaction when we are treated "unjustly." He "finds favor" with us when we humble ourselves and patiently accept undeserved, harsh treatment. You are "blessed" when you are "reviled for the name of Christ…because the Spirit of glory and of God rests on you." You are "blessed" when you "suffer for the sake of righteousness." Lastly, "It is better…we suffer for doing what is right rather than for doing what is wrong."

Rather than be aghast with the thought of being unjustly accused, we can be extremely grateful the persecution we may be experiencing isn't caused by something we've done. Moreover, God's grace has kept us from wrongdoing and has spared us from disgracing our Lord and ourselves! Suffering for doing right is painful, but the rewards for well-doing far outreach the consequences of sin and its resulting shame.

We should also look at one of the principles of being a follower of Christ. Jesus has often been called the 'Pattern Son.' He walked this earth as a man—even though He was God. He was filled with the Spirit and dependent on the Father, as an example for us to follow. We will experience much of what He experienced, and our lives will often follow the pattern of His life. He identified with our humanity, and we must be willing to identify with His life, death, burial, resurrection, and ascension.

This principle applies to 1 Peter 3:18. Christ, "the just," died for us, "the unjust." His death was the ultimate sacrifice. The One Who was never guilty of any wrongdoing died for us, who in the words of Isaiah, "have become like one who is unclean, And all our righteous deeds are like a filthy garment; And all of us wither like a leaf, And our iniquities, like the wind, take us away" (Isaiah 64:6).

The next time we are unjustly treated, we need to put things into perspective by comparing Christ's perfection to our record of 'being and doing right.' Then, consider our 'suffering' with the pain Jesus experienced. He was "despised and rejected by men, A Man of sorrows and acquainted with grief" (Isaiah 53:3). Ultimately, He hung on a cross to die—the sinless One for sinners like us.

Count It All Joy

My brethren, count it all joy when you fall into various trials, knowing that the testing of your faith produces patience. But let patience have its perfect work, that you may be perfect and complete, lacking nothing. (James 1:2–4)

Blessed [happy, to be envied] is the man who is patient under trial and stands up under temptation, for when he has stood the test and been approved, he will receive [the victor's] crown of life which God has promised to those who love Him. (James 1:12, AMPC)

We consistently hear reports from all over the world of brothers and sisters in Christ rejoicing over the opportunity to suffer or be martyred for their faith. These same believers are saddened—actually sickened—by the carnality and self-centered mind-set of Christians in North America.

In order for us to rejoice over the thought of being persecuted for the Lord's sake, our minds must be renewed to think as the mind of Christ. Not only do we not think as He does, but our watered-down version of the gospel has created a climate of apathy—even in the evangelical churches of America. It is time to unapologetically return to the gospel of the Kingdom!

The Gospel of the Kingdom

The church of Jesus Christ has suffered persecution from its inception. As soon as Jesus began teaching contrary to the religious leaders of His day, great opposition arose against Him and all who followed in His way. When He declared the Kingdom of God had come to earth through His incarnation, the leaders of organized religion of His day wanted to kill Him. Those who are driven by their flesh and energized by the enemy of our souls will do anything to silence the truth about the One Who is, "the way, and the truth, and the life" (John 14:6).

Revelation 12 gives a vivid picture of this truth. Immediately upon Jesus' birth, the Red Dragon is positioned to devour the "man child" (Revelation 12:5, KJV)—long before His public ministry even began! This battle between the Kingdom of Darkness and the Kingdom of Light was laid out from the beginning of time in God's curse upon the serpent in the Garden of Eden.

> And I will put enmity between you and the woman, and between your seed and her seed; He shall bruise you on the head, And you shall bruise him on the heel. (Genesis 3:15)

With this curse upon him, Satan knew his only hope to rule the earth was to make sure the "seed" of the woman was destroyed. It is no coincidence that throughout history Satan has inspired desperate leaders to order the mass killing of male babies, with the intent of stopping "the male child" from ever reaching maturity. This is clearly illustrated in scripture by Satan's initial assault against this "man child" when he inspired King Herod to order the slaughter of all males, two years of age and under, in a diabolical attempt to destroy the King of the Jews (Matthew 2:16).

The purpose of laying this foundation is to make your position in Christ clear. The day you accepted Jesus as Savior, you became part of Christ's body and Satan became the enemy of your soul. In America—due to lack of persecution—we have been able to accept Jesus as Savior and go on with life pretty much as usual. In addition, the difference between simply being born again and being a disciple of Christ is rarely taught, let alone emphasized. Nonetheless, the bible unmistakably teaches the distinction between the two.

> Then Jesus said to His disciples, "If anyone wishes to come after Me, he must deny himself, and take up his cross and follow Me. For whoever wishes to save his life will lose it; but whoever loses his life for My sake will find it. For what will it profit a man if he gains the whole world and forfeits his soul? Or what will a man give in exchange for his soul?" (Matthew 16:24–26)

In most parts of the world, the gospel of the Kingdom is this: "If you make a public profession of faith in Jesus Christ, including, but not limited to, public water baptism, your life will never be the same." You may be martyred on the spot, your family may be tortured in an attempt to coerce you into denying your faith in Christ, you may lose your job and, in many countries (especially Muslim countries), you may never be able to find work again simply because you are a Christian. The list of instant, satanic-inspired attacks against you could be long and gruesome. Satan has one agenda, and that is "to steal and kill and destroy" (John 10:10).

Many, if not most, of the preachers and teachers in America have presented a "seeker-friendly/prosperity gospel" that—at best—produces weak and often disillusioned Christians. One time, as I asked the Lord about such teaching, He spoke very clearly to my heart, "It's not My gospel!" I believe that says it all. Jesus, Himself, spoke very clearly about what following Him would require.

> If the world hates you, you know that it has hated Me before it hated you. If you were of the world, the world would love its own; but because you are not of the world, but I chose you out of the world, because of this the world hates you. Remember the word that I said to you, "A slave is not greater than his master.' If they persecuted Me, they will also persecute you; if they kept My word, they will keep yours also." (John 15:18–20)

> Beloved, do not be surprised at the fiery ordeal among you, which comes upon you for your testing, as though some strange thing were happening to you; but to the degree that you share the sufferings of Christ, keep on rejoicing, so that also at the revelation of His glory you may rejoice with exultation. (1 Peter 4:12–13)

One of the main reasons we don't "count it all joy" (James 1:2) when trials come is because we were taught something other than the gospel of Christ. Jesus clearly taught us to expect to be treated in the same way He was treated. The true gospel teaches us to expect tribulation in this world, while at the same time knowing we are destined to overcome every obstacle! A great disservice has been done to the body of Christ by avoiding the 'hard teachings' of scripture in our teaching and preaching. We often leave out the parts we think no one wants to hear, and because of this, we have left our young recruits unprepared for battle. If we taught the truth of what following Christ is really like, no one would be surprised when confronted by trials and tribulation. We would have an army enlisted with the expectation of doing battle in the name of the Lover of their Souls and persecution would be an honor!

It is very clear in the New Testament that 'the norm' for followers of Christ was to not only persevere under great persecution but to rejoice in the midst of it. One such account, preserved in scripture as an encouragement to us, is found in Acts 16. Paul and Silas had been led by the Holy Spirit to the Roman province of Macedonia to preach the gospel. During their time in Macedonia, a slave-girl with a spirit of divination followed them and called out after them for many days. Finally, annoyed by the demonic spirit controlling her, Paul rebuked the spirit and she was set free. Since she had been making a lot of money for her master through divination, her master grabbed Paul and Silas and brought them before the authorities with false accusations. Although Paul was a Roman citizen and had a legal right to complain, he chose to not demand his rights. He and Silas were beaten with rods and thrown into the "inner prison." It is common belief the "inner prison" was the lowest level where the sewage drained. This unimaginable scenario is where we find one of the most glorious examples of 'right thinking' under unjust persecution.

> But about midnight Paul and Silas were praying and singing hymns of praise to God, and the prisoners were listening to them. (Acts 16:25)

The surrender of Paul's rights as a Roman citizen paved the way for them to be in a place where their witness of praying and praising God—in the worst of conditions—could result in the salvation of many souls and in the gospel being firmly established in Macedonia. Never forget, rejoicing with thanksgiving, while under persecution, is an exceptionally powerful witness. Such a response is not natural but is a supernatural manifestation of the divine nature within us.

The Proof of Your Faith

The world is always watching to see if we live what we say we believe. This fact is evidenced by the media explosion that results from the moral failure of any prominent Christian. Although the world is looking to find fault in us as an excuse to reject the teachings of the bible, scripture does exhort us to live lives that are "proof" of our faith.

Consider it wholly joyful, my brethren, whenever you are enveloped in or encounter trials of any sort or fall into various temptations. Be assured and understand that the trial and proving of your faith bring out endurance and steadfastness and patience. But let endurance and steadfastness and patience have full play and do a thorough work, so that you may be perfectly and fully developed [with no defects], lacking in nothing. (James 1:2–4, AMPC)

And not only that, but we also rejoice in our afflictions, because we know that affliction produces endurance, endurance produces proven character, and proven character produces hope. This hope does not disappoint, because God's love has been poured out in our hearts through the Holy Spirit who was given to us. (Romans 5:3–5, HCSB)

The principle of 'no pain, no gain' is touted throughout society as necessary for success. In the world of sports, in countless other competitions, in a passion for fame, and in the everyday disciplines of life, some work tirelessly to perfect their skills. Yet, in the case of spiritual disciplines, few Christians persevere for any length of time. Worse yet, many never even get started! Our faith will never be strong enough to be proof of the reality of Jesus Christ within us until we choose to rejoice in the trials and temptations of life and thank God for these opportunities to give Him glory.

It is really very straightforward. We simply have to see the quality of our spiritual walk as more valuable than fame or fortune of any kind—more important than the fulfillment of our wildest dreams.

There really is no comparison if we are 'thinking right.' After all, our spiritual "endurance and steadfastness and patience" is of eternal value—all else is temporal. Just imagine the impact—not on just our own walk—but on the lives we will touch in a lifetime when we choose to walk uprightly.

There is only one way in life to develop endurance, and that is to progressively go beyond the point of comfort in order to gain new ground. Repeating this process over and over again strengthens us and produces endurance not obtainable in any other way. For this reason, we can rejoice when the trials of life give us opportunity to press beyond our previous breaking point.

In the darkest times of our lives, we have opportunity for great spiritual advancement, which may never again be repeated. In those places, we need to embrace our problems with great gusto and ask the Lord, "What do You want me to do with this?" These moments are not as common as we think, and our attitude and choices during times of crisis are crucial in shaping our destiny. In seasons of intense trial, God is determining what He can trust us to do and what we are prepared to endure!

Do you cooperate with God's dealings with you? The apostle James was well-aware of the bottom line of usefulness for God (spiritual success): "That the trial and proving of your faith bring out endurance and steadfastness and patience. But (it is your choice to) let endurance and steadfastness and patience have full play and do a thorough work, so that you may be perfectly and fully developed [with no defects], lacking in nothing." Our attitude toward the 'unpleasant things' of life is everything!

One last comment regarding the proof of our faith comes from a word picture in Romans 5:4. This text shows the need to have the mind of Christ when under persecution, in order to be "proof" to an unbelieving world. This verse states, "endurance produces proven character." The picture of "proven character" is similar to the process used to produce tempered steel. Tempering is a heat treatment used to toughen steel from its original brittle (easily broken, quick to fall apart) state. The steel is transformed into a new form that is tough and ductile, ductile being defined as:

1. Malleable enough to be worked: able to be drawn out into wire or hammered into very thin sheets.
2. Readily shaped: able to be molded or shaped without breaking.
3. Readily influenced: easily persuaded or influenced. [32]

The refining fire of the Lord heats us, in order to transform us from our brittle, carnal nature into one that is tough and "malleable enough to be worked." If we continue to cooperate with the Lord in this superhot refining fire, we will also become pliable and become capable of being "readily shaped" into the image of Christ. The end of this tempering process leaves us with "proven character," conditioned to be "readily influenced" by the Lord to do His will, in His way, and in His time.

> In this you greatly rejoice, even though now for a little while, if necessary, you have been distressed by various trials, so that the proof of your faith, being more precious than gold which is perishable, even though tested by fire, may be found to result in praise and glory and honor at the revelation of Jesus Christ. (1 Peter 1:6–7)

Sam Storm's comments on this verse are worth repeating: "Trials are grievous… Let no one pretend they are anything less than painful and distressing. But there is always a divine design in our suffering that, when seen and embraced, energizes the heart to persevere."[33]

An Expected End to Suffering

> [As] an example of suffering and ill-treatment together with patience, brethren, take the prophets who spoke in the name of the Lord [as His messengers]. You know how we call those blessed [happy] who were steadfast [who endured]. You have

---

[32.] Encarta World English Dictionary
[33.] Sam Storms. *To the One Who Conquers.* pg. 59.

heard of the endurance of Job, and you have seen the Lord's [purpose and how He richly blessed him in the] end, inasmuch as the Lord is full of pity and compassion and tenderness and mercy. (James 5:10–11, AMPC)

We can rejoice in suffering, since allowed to do "its perfect work," the result will be our becoming "perfect and complete, lacking nothing." God has one plan and His intention is to set us free from the tyranny of our self-centered flesh and to transform us into the likeness of His glory. In the admonition of the late Kelley Varner, "Stop kicking against the very thing that God has provided to set you free. God knows what He is doing."[34]

The wilderness was the place of punishment for Israel's unbelief and consequent disobedience. The term "wilderness" is still used today to represent extended periods of discipline, testing, trial and pressure. Never forget, God has a master plan and knows exactly what He is doing!

Remember how the LORD your God led you through the wilderness for these forty years, humbling you and testing you to prove your character, and to find out whether or not you would obey His commands. (Deuteronomy 8:2)

Again, from Kelley Varner: "The Father knows what we are becoming. He sees the end from the beginning. He wants us to see and to know ourselves as He sees and knows us. The wilderness is necessary. There are no options or shortcuts. We will never know how strong we are in God until we have been proven."[35] There is an expected end to suffering!

In his epistle, James reminds us that in our seasons of suffering, "the Lord is full of pity and compassion and tenderness and mercy." We can have deep peace and joy in the midst of trials, knowing the God of the universe is always watching over us and preparing us for

---

[34.] Kelley Varner. *Prevail: A Handbook for the Overcomer.* pg. 124.
[35.] ibid

His best. He can, however, only use us and bless us when we have proven faithful to His calling. James used the lives of the prophets of old as examples of those who remained steadfast under persecution. He made a special point of identifying Job as an example of endurance, who—due to his faithfulness—God "richly blessed" in the end.

Meditate on one last encouraging word from Sam Storms:

Suffering isn't designed by God to destroy our faith but to intensify it. That will never happen, however, if we fail to look beyond the pain to the purpose of our Heavenly Father. His design is to knock out from underneath us every false prop so that we might rely wholly on Him. His aim is to create in us such desperation that we have nowhere else to look but to His promises and abiding presence.[36]

Looking at the words of Sam Storms, one key to joy in the midst of suffering is "to look beyond the pain to the purpose of our Heavenly Father." Although we may not know our Heavenly Father's plan, we can always be assured it is for our good.

"For I know the plans I have for you," says the LORD. "They are plans for good and not for disaster, to give you a future and a hope." (Jeremiah 29:11, NLT)

Bless Your Persecutors—Pray for Them

You have heard that it was said, "You shall love your neighbor and hate your enemy." But I say to you, love your enemies and pray for those who persecute you. (Matthew 5:43–44)

Even as there is great power in rejoicing while under persecution, there is also great power in forgiving your persecutors! When you choose to forgive and earnestly pray for the very ones who persecute

---

[36.] Sam Storms. *To the One Who Conquers.* pg. 60.

you, you will actually begin to love them. I can tell you from years of experience, if you quickly follow the pattern of forgiveness, prayer, and love, it is possible to walk in peace in the midst of persecution.

When we respond to persecution according to scripture, there is also a dimension of great power released toward the offender. I have heard many amazing testimonies of miraculous results in the lives of persecutors when victims have responded God's way. When a victim openly expresses forgiveness and God's love to the offender, a great grace for repentance is released into the life of the offender. This often results in the offender throwing himself/herself upon the mercy of God and receiving Christ as Savior—without any previous knowledge of the gospel!

A witness of this truth—that treating offenders God's way releases a grace for repentance—is found in Romans 12.

> Never take your own revenge, beloved, but leave room for the wrath of God, for it is written, "Vengeance is Mine, I will repay," says the Lord. "But if your enemy is hungry, feed him, and if he is thirsty, give him a drink; For in so doing you will heap burning coals on his head." Do not be overcome by evil, but overcome evil with good. (Romans 12:19–21)

At first reading, this text would seem to suggest you would be getting even with your enemy by heaping burning coals upon his head. This would not be consistent with the first part of the verse, however, where God says to leave vengeance to Him. Romans 12:20 is actually a quote of Proverbs 25:21–22, which reads, "You will heap burning coals on his head," and is actually a metaphor taken from smelting metals. When smelting, ore is put into the furnace. Fire is put both under the ore and over it in order to liquefy the ore, remove the dross, and purify the metal. This word picture is actually illustrating 'heaping kindness' on the person. When this is done toward an offender, there will be a release of grace with the purpose of melting the heart of the offender, bringing repentance, and enabling restitution.

Another common thought on this text identifies it as a Jewish figure of speech.

> In the Bible lands almost everything is carried on the head—water jars, baskets of fruit, vegetables, fish or any other article. Those carrying the burden rarely touch it with the hands, and they walk through crowded streets and lanes with perfect ease. In many homes the only fire they have is kept in a *brazier,* which they use for simple cooking as well as for warmth. They plan to always keep it burning. If it should go out, some member of the family will take the brazier to a neighbor's house to borrow fire.
>
> Then she will lift the brazier to her head and start for home. If her neighbor is a generous woman, she will heap the brazier full of coals. To feed an enemy and give him drink was like heaping the empty brazier with live coals—which meant food, warmth and almost life itself to the person or home needing it, and was the symbol of finest generosity.[37]

Regardless of the exact origin of the phrase "heap burning coals on his head," it is definitely symbolic of heaping such kindness upon our enemies that the grace of God—released by our obedience—would lead them to repentance. Our forgiveness, prayer, and love for our enemies is a picture of the love and forgiveness we received when we were still the "enemy of God" (James 4:4).

If God Is for Us, Who Is against Us?

> What then shall we say to these things? If God is for us, who is against us? He who did not spare His own Son, but delivered Him over for us all, how will He not also with Him freely give us all things? Who will bring a charge against God's elect? God

---

[37.] B.M. Bowen. *Strange Scriptures that Perplex the Western Mind.*

is the one who justifies; who is the one who condemns? Christ Jesus is He who died, yes, rather who was raised, who is at the right hand of God, who also intercedes for us. Who will separate us from the love of Christ? Will tribulation, or distress, or persecution, or famine, or nakedness, or peril, or sword? Just as it is written, "For Your sake we are being put to death all day long; We were considered as sheep to be slaughtered." But in all these things we overwhelmingly conquer through Him who loved us. For I am convinced that neither death, nor life, nor angels, nor principalities, nor things present, nor things to come, nor powers, nor height, nor depth, nor any other created thing, will be able to separate us from the love of God, which is in Christ Jesus our Lord. (Romans 8:31–39)

In order to feel blessed in the midst of persecution, we must think like God thinks. With regards to persecution, the bible teaches several pivotal truths we need to know, internalize, and embrace.

- First, God is for us—at all times—and He is all-powerful. "Who is against us?" really means, who can stand against Almighty God? The emphatic answer to this question is nothing or no one!
- Second, He who gave the life of His only Son for our freedom will, through the Son, give us all things; "seeing that His divine power has granted to us everything pertaining to life and godliness, through the true knowledge of Him who called us by His own glory and excellence" (2 Peter 1:3).
- Third, who can get away with making a charge against God's elect when it is Christ Jesus Himself who continually makes intercession for us? Again, the answer is an emphatic nothing or no one!
- Fourth, "Who [or what] will separate us from the love of Christ?" This question is answered by implication. Nothing on the list of "things we hope never happen to us" can separate us from the love of Christ! We need "to comprehend

with all the saints what is the breadth and length and height and depth, and to know the love of Christ which surpasses knowledge, that (we) may be filled up to all the fullness of God" (Ephesians 3:18–19). With this understanding comes great confidence and ever-increasing faith.

- Fifth, "But in all these things we overwhelmingly conquer through Him who loved us." Christ's victory at the cross is the guarantee of our victory. Meditate on these verses:

But thanks be to God, who gives us the victory through our Lord Jesus Christ. (1 Corinthians 15:57)

But thanks be to God, who always leads us in triumph in Christ, and manifests through us the sweet aroma of the knowledge of Him in every place. (2 Corinthians 2:14)

For whatever is born of God overcomes the world; and this is the victory that has overcome the world—our faith. (1 John 5:4)

We need never fear persecution since, as Christians, God is on our side and nothing can touch us apart from the lifting of His hand. He never wastes our pain and always has our best interest at heart. There is never a time when He is not closely watching over us, directing us, and fulfilling the dreams He has given us.

As we walk through the trials and tribulations of this life, His grace will always be sufficient. Just like a good marriage, the more we go through with our Beloved, the sweeter the relationship becomes. Oh, what an honor it is that we could be called "sons of the living God" (Romans 9:23-26).

All of heaven and earth are anxiously waiting and watching for the day when the Lord of the universe reveals His glorious church to the powers that have ruled this earth for far too long (Ephesians 3:10). What a glorious day, when those who choose to overcome will play a part in the establishment of the Kingdom of Heaven on earth.

In the light of all we are and all we have been given in Christ, we should be encouraged to willingly suffer persecution in this life, to prove what we're really made of. At the time of Christ, the name "Christian" was first used as a derogatory term describing those who followed Christ. In fact, one reference states that "Christian" literally means, "little Christs." The world again needs to see those who walk so closely to their Master that they are called "little Christs." Our response to our persecutors, to those who despitefully use us, and to our enemies, could just be the witness that will draw many to the One Whose name we bear!

APPENDIX 1

Confession of Sin

Our traditional understanding of 1 John 1:9 leads us away from the simplicity of the gospel.

> If we confess our sins, He is faithful and righteous to forgive us our sins and to cleanse us from all unrighteousness. (1 John 1:9)

The word translated twice as "sins" in the *New American Standard Bible* in 1 John 1:9 is found in the *Strong's Exhaustive Concordance* under number 266, *"hamartia."* According to the *Vine's Expository Dictionary, "hamartia"* is in the noun form. In other words, it is not used in the sense of "missing the mark" in a specific committal of an act of sin or in the verb sense of sinning but is spoken of as a principle of sin. It is referring to the inward element that produces the acts or the power acting through the body. This is in reference to the sinful nature.

We know that when we receive Christ as our Savior, we are crucified with Him "in order that our body of sin might be done away with, so that we would no longer be slaves to sin; for he who has died is freed from sin" (Romans 6:6–7). Subsequently, in reference to 1 John 1:9, if we confess the fact that we are a sinner—unable to do anything but sin because of the sinful nature we inherited from Adam—He will forgive us of our sinfulness. This verse is a description of salvation, not the need for continual confession.

When we are born again, we receive the nature of Christ and are cleansed from all unrighteousness.

> He made Him who knew no sin to be sin on our behalf, so that we might become the righteousness of God in Him. (2 Corinthians 5:21)

> So that He (Jesus) might sanctify (purify or consecrate) her (the church), having cleansed her by the washing of water with the word, that He might present to Himself the church in all her glory, having no spot or wrinkle or any such thing; but that she would be holy and blameless. (Ephesians 5:26–27, author's comments)

I John 1:9 is speaking of our initial need of confessing our inherent unrighteousness and our need for a Savior. Since our spirit-man is made righteous through identification with Christ Jesus, there is no state of sinfulness (noun) to confess for a person who is already in Christ.

Even if we are diligent in trying to ask for forgiveness for any known sin, there could still remain unconfessed sins of omission or sins unknown to us. We may have made unrighteous judgments, have said unloving words, or have heart attitudes we did not consider sin. If confession were necessary for forgiveness, the fact that these sins were unknown to us would not change our state of unrighteousness before a holy God. Our eternal security would then be based on what we have done and not on the finished work of Jesus Christ.

The truth, however, is that if our daily sins were never confessed, we would still be righteous in the eyes of our Heavenly Father. The blood of Jesus continually cleanses us from all unrighteousness—even when we have not asked for forgiveness. Confession has several purposes in the life of a believer, but it is not the requisite for the forgiveness of our sins through the application of the blood of Jesus.

It is true, when we have unconfessed sin in our lives, our sin is not 'under the blood' and we are not in the 'place of immunity.' Our yielding to unrighteousness gives the enemy legal ground to assault us. This not only gives permission for Satan to send a harvest into our lives based on what we have sown, but the word tells us, "they sow the wind and they reap the whirlwind" (Hosea 8:7).

> For the one who sows to his own flesh will from the flesh reap corruption, but the one who sows to the Spirit will from the Spirit reap eternal life. (Galatians 6:8)

"Corruption" is a decline in the quality of life, and "eternal life" is Christ's life or abundant life. Confession does not change our standing with God the Father, who sees us with the righteous nature of His Son. Nonetheless, unconfessed sin does cause "corruption," which is a decline in the quality of life.

Unconfessed sin also hinders our confidence with God. When we have unconfessed sin in our lives, we are like the little boy who just took a cookie out of the cookie jar without permission. When his mother enters the room, he puts the hand with the cookie in it behind him and stands back, rather than running into her arms. When we feel dirty, we are unlikely to "draw near with confidence to the throne of grace, so that we may receive mercy and find grace to help in time of need" (Hebrews 4:16). Unconfessed sin will often condemn us into running from our only hope for freedom from our guilt and shame. Since we withdraw from the Father's presence and do not avail ourselves to His grace, this condition can lead to a very dangerous downward spiral.

The last purpose for the confession of sin is our need to agree with a holy God that we have transgressed His will. Unless we confess our sin, we are not acknowledging our need for our Father's grace to overcome the character flaw that led to our transgression. Confession of sin is a part of our transformation into the image of Christ. If we confess our sin, which is agreeing with God that we have missed the mark, then we are acknowledging our need for His grace, which is our only hope for permanent change.

The Bottom Line

Although the daily confession of sin is not necessary for forgiveness, all three of the above reasons for confessing our sins affect the intimacy of our relationship with our Father. The preciousness of this relationship is far too valuable to let unconfessed sin remain in our lives. One definition of the "fear of God" is "the awesome dread of displeasing Him." Nothing on this earth—no attitude in our heart—is worth the disruption of the peace, joy, and sense of security of an unhindered relationship with the One Who loves us most!

"In each generation God moves forward to the culmination of His purpose for the church in the earth. In each generation God reveals more truth that has been hidden in the word from man's understanding."
—Ruth Herzer

"We desperately need to understand that we live in the Kingdom of God now, on this earth. The kingdom is an invisible realm, which although not seen, is more real than anything we can see with our natural eyes. The Kingdom of Heaven is not a far off place, but a spiritual dimension in which we already live, through our relationship with Jesus Christ."
—*Kingdom Life*, Intro

Heaven is not "heaven" because of a specific location but is "heaven" due to the presence of God. The presence of God in Eden allowed the Father to fellowship with His creation. The increase of His presence on earth will bring the atmosphere of 'heaven' to earth, which will eventually make *"all things new."*
—*Kingdom Life*

"God's primary concern is not where we go when we die, but what kingdom we choose to live in today— eternity is a byproduct of that choice."
—*Kingdom Life*, Intro

To arrange conferences, speaking engagements or book signing events, please contact info@newlifeoutreach.us. Rhonda's publications also include *The Exchanged Life-The Revelation of Jesus Christ in You.* Coming soon in the *Kingdom Life* Series: *Establishing the Kingdom of Heaven on Earth.*

About the Author

Rhonda J. Mead is an ordained minister, Christian writer, and speaker. Her passion for over 30 years has been sharing and teaching biblical principles for personal freedom and an overcoming life through the power of the cross. Rhonda appeared on the TCT Network's *Ask the Pastor* program for over 19 years, as well as on her locally produced program, *Rhonda from the Heart.*

Rhonda and her husband, Richard, serve as co-directors of New Life Outreach, a nonprofit ministry based out of Holton, Michigan. It is through this global outreach that Rhonda and Richard work to share the message of personal and regional transformation through the power of the cross.

CPSIA information can be obtained
at www.ICGtesting.com
Printed in the USA
JSHW041921060621
15627JS00001B/3

9 781098 055271